A Bite-Size

Oil Dorado

Guyana's Black Gold

Edited by
John Mair and Neil Fowler

Published by Bite-Sized Books Ltd 2019

Bite-Sized Books Ltd Cleeve Croft, Cleeve Road, Goring RG8 9BJ UK
information@bite-sizedbooks.com
Registered in the UK. Company Registration No: 9395379

Bite-Sized Books Ltd Cleeve Croft, Cleeve Road, Goring RG8 9BJ UK
information@bite-sizedbooks.com
Registered in the UK. Company Registration No: 9395379
ISBN: 9781798909355

Acknowledgements

These books are always acorns that become oak trees through team enterprise. The book was John Mair's idea just five weeks before publication. It derived from an interview session he conducted with Dr Mark Bynoe of the Guyana Department of Energy in January 2019 by Skype from Georgetown to London. Thanks to him and to High Commissioner Hamley Case for facilitating that event.

The idea became reality through the 16 authors who have written and delivered to a very tight deadline for no fee. We are eternally grateful to them.

The future of Guyana and oil is important to all of us. This book is a deliberate *pot pourri* of economics, politics, futurology and literature. It aims to reflect the rich cultural and intellectual heritage of Guyana and kick start the long overdue debate on just how El Dorado will accommodate Black Gold.

Let reading and argument begin.

John Mair, Oxford
Neil Fowler, Northumberland

The Editors

John Mair was born in the then British Guiana (to an 'Old Guianese' mother) in 1950. He went to Sacred Heart RC School in Georgetown. John won the top scholarship in the Common Entrance exam in Guiana in 1961.Then his parents emigrated to the UK. He returns regularly to Guyana.

John has taught journalism at the Universities of Coventry, Kent, Northampton, Brunel, Edinburgh Napier, Guyana and the Communication University of China. He has edited 30 'hackademic' volumes over the last ten years on subjects ranging from trust in television, the health of investigative journalism, reporting the Arab Spring, to three volumes on the Leveson Inquiry. He also created the Coventry Conversations, which attracted 350 media movers and shakers to Coventry University; the podcasts of those have been downloaded six million times worldwide. Since then, he has launched the Northampton Chronicles, Media Mondays at Napier and most recently the Harrow Conversations at Westminster University. In a previous life, he was an award-winning producer/director for the BBC, ITV and Channel 4, and a secondary school teacher.

Neil Fowler has been in journalism since graduation, starting life as trainee reporter on the Leicester Mercury. He went on to edit four regional dailies, including The Journal in the north east of England and The Western Mail in Wales. He was then publisher of The Toronto Sun in Canada before returning to the UK to edit Which? magazine. In 2010/11 he was the Guardian Research Fellow at Oxford University's Nuffield College where he investigated the decline and future of regional and local newspapers in the UK. From then until 2016 he helped organise the college's prestigious David Butler media and politics seminars. He remains an associate member of Nuffield. As well as being an occasional contributor to trade magazines he now acts as an adviser to organisations on their management and their external and internal communications and media policies and strategies.

Contents

Poem: Oil

John Agard

Gushing from earth's abundance
a dream of black gold

to eel your way through fingers
coaxing a glow out of skin

or simply playing your role
of a sizzling puddle in a pan.

A little of you, says the hymn,
will keep a lamp burning

till the break of day. *Sing
hosanna sing.*

Yet, the ever slick one,
you anoint a prophet's brow

as well as the wheels of war.
Oil, whose side are you on?

About the contributor

John Agard, born and educated in Georgetown, Guyana, is the author of a number of books for adults and young readers. For his collection *Man to Pan*, inspired by the evolution of the steel pan, he was awarded the Casa de las Americas Poetry Prize. Twice winner of the Guyana Prize, he was BBC poet-in-residence in 1998 and received the Queen's Gold Medal for Poetry in 2012.

Black gold in a Green economy

Foreword by Moses V. Nagamootoo
Prime Minister and Minister of Public Information

As this hitherto unknown country, re-named the Co-operative Republic of Guyana from its colonial appellation "British Guiana", approaches its Golden Jubilee as a Republic, its new image as the promising major oil producer is that of the fabled El Dorado – the lost city of gold.

With a population of less than one million people, mostly descendants of African slaves and Indian Indentured labourers who were once tied to the British colonial sugar plantocracy, Guyana is today a hot point for industry projections and opinions.

Its numerous, huge off-shore oil finds started in 2015. The ExxonMobil-led consortium - Exxon, HESS and CNOOC Petroleum - has announced "First Oil" in the coming months. With two huge new discoveries, the number of wells has increased to 12 in only one area – the Stabroek Block, which is some 120 km within Guyana's EEZ.

Exxon has said that there is potential for at least five floating production storage and offloading vessels that can produce more than 750,000 barrels of oil per day by 2025! That has influenced one American writer, Steve LeVine, in an article titled, "*The surprising next oil superpower*", to describe Guyana as being "on the cusp of becoming one of the world's wealthiest nations". LeVine projected that at US$60 a barrel, he added, Guyana could receive more than US$5 billion a year in revenue.

The Norwegian Consultant, Rystad Energy, estimates that Guyana stands to earn more than $6 Billion in royalties and taxes annually by the end of 2020. With the significant amount of money expected to flow to Guyana, the Government has begun serious planning on how to utilise the expected oil resources to benefit all our people. The Government has crafted a solid legal framework to protect our oil and gas wealth under a Natural Resources Fund Act - Guyana's version of a Sovereign Wealth Fund.

Further, investment in infrastructures and spending on social services, including education, health and housing, will be guided by rigid fiscal rules as well as the Guyana Green State Development Strategy (GSDS). Meanwhile, the Guyana National Upstream Oil and Gas Policy and a Local Content Policy have been finalised.

To update and develop its policies, regulations and legislation, Guyana has received support from several countries and organisations: the United Nations Development Programme (UNDP), the World Bank, United States, Kingdom of Norway, Trinidad and Tobago, World Wildlife Fund, European Union, Canada, Chile, Mexico, the Russian Federation and Conservation International (CI).

Effective management of the oil and gas sector is crucial to its success. Towards this aim an Energy Department has been established under the auspices of the Ministry of the Presidency, while a Petroleum Department has been added to the Ministry of Natural Resources. Upon the passage of a Petroleum Commission Bill, a broad-based Commission will be established to regulate the oil and gas sector to ensure that the interests of the people of Guyana are protected.

Introduction

Leading with local content

John Mair

This book is a labour of love; a festschrift to my mother's land and that of her mothers, her grandmothers and great grandmothers before her.

I was born in the then British Guiana to an 'old Guianese' family. I go back 'home' frequently and have seen it develop from an impoverished state- second only to Haiti in HIPC terms – brains drained to the USA, Canada and the UK, through the false rebirth as a narco economy trans-shipping 'white gold', cocaine, from Colombia to the USA and Europe though the long slow death of the sugar industry (in which I was brought up) – to the light at the end of the tunnel. A huge booming oil economy to definitely come. This collection is a necessary *pot pourri* of literature, economics but mostly hope, as we start with a poem by Jon Agard

But first. the fantasy. Christopher Minster in **'Sir Walter Raleigh and El Dorado: the myth traced to source** ' looks at how or more than 500 years the quest for El Dorado, the mythical city of gold in South America/Guiana has persisted. Nobody has ever found it – even the original explorer. He concludes: 'Today, Sir Walter Raleigh is remembered for many things, including his writings and his participation in the 1596 attack on the Spanish port of Cadiz, but he will forever be associated with the vain quest for El Dorado'.

That fantasy reverberates in the literature of Guyana over decades. No more so than in the work of Sir Wilson Harris the most mystic, some say muddy, of her great writers. He spent his early life in the Guyanese interior – the land of El Dorado. His modern Boswell is Dr Michael Mitchell of the University of Warwick.

In **'El Dorado in the Work of Wilson Harris'** he explores the possible thoughts of Wilson Harris – what would one of Guyana's greatest writers have made of black gold? The answer is that he would have said *Be careful what you wish for*.

9

Indranie Deolall, Guyanese writer, in **The oil** *baccoo* looks to oil as the modern incarnation of a traditional manifestation The *baccoo* is "an active, wicked spirit believed to take the form of some small, living, partly human being that must be kept in a bottle and may be commanded either to bring its owner great wealth or to do harm to other persons". Thereby lies the rub.

Back the real, material world, Sally Gibson of Petro Legal and John Mair, outline **'Guyana's oil discoveries to date'**. They look at just how much oil there is. They outline the progress of the search for the new black gold in just one field to date. The answer is five billion barrels and counting more by the day. It could easily double. The oil just keeps coming and it is relatively easy and relatively cheap to find.

Some are already getting their hands oily, Charles Cosad, an oil industry veteran now with Totaltec looks at **'A nation with ambition at its heart'**. In a startling stat he predicts that Guyana will be producing one barrel of oil per head of population on 2025!

Riches round the corner

Christopher Ram, Guyanese attorney and accountant, is an iconoclast. He is a sage and sceptic on the oil industry. Week after week in his column in the *Stabroek News* he has poured cold water on troubled oil. In **'A new age dawns, finally'** he has a positive conclusion; 'The clues were there but it has taken decades of hope – and border disputes – for oil to be finally realised', Ram says.

Robert Persaud is the nearly man. He is former Minister of Natural Resources in Guyana. He lost office in March 2015. Exxon announced its first discovery in May 2015. Robert would also like to have been the PPP President. That was and is not to be. In **'Is Guyana ready for prime time?'** he looks forward to the future rather than dwelling on the past. "Oil will be ours to determine whether it will be a curse or cure," he says, "and I'm confident it will be one of the many cures to our decades-old social and economic setbacks. The work of attaining the elusive goal of national prosperity has now started with the beckoning of oil and gas!"

Expertise is at a premium. You can count the lawyers with oil knowledge in Guyana on one hand. Well four fingers. All have studied at Aberdeen University and Sanjeev Datadin, Guyanese attorney, is one. In **'Is the law up to it'? The need for parliamentary oversight'** he explores the missteps in early petro law making which should not be repeated if Guyana is to reap all the potential benefits of its new oil resource. "Only an established legal and regulatory framework can achieve this in a fair way. The alternative can be disastrous". he concludes

Sally Gibson was born in Guyana but raised in the UK where she practices. Her legal experience is global over four decades. In **'The case for a Petroleum Commission'** she says Guyana stands on the cusp of amazing transformational change. One that it cannot afford to flunk. "As an emerging producer, Guyana possesses a vast amount of political and social energy. The hope is that it will be able to harness this whilst maintaining the balance between openness and effectiveness."

My long-term interest in Guyana oil is explored in a paper which I presented at the Society For Caribbean Studies in London in July 2018. In **'El Dorado in Danger? Will oil make or ruin Guyana?The Lessons from Trinidad'**, I explore the lessons for Guyana from others especially Trinidad and Tobago which has been in the oil game for over a century. Its days of glory have passed and I suggest "Guyana is a neophyte oil power. The gush of discoveries has been relentless and swift. The country has to play 'catch up' on all fronts with some speed. Trinidad and Tobago provides some directions-positive and negative-for the way forward."

It is worth noting that the audience for that paper was just five people – many more were discussing 'Post Colonial Literature' in all its aspects. Misguided?

Guyana's nearest neighbour Venezuela is in a state of permanent chaos. President Maduro presides over hyper inflation that puts Weimar Germany in the shade and what looks like the first stirrings of a civil war.

In **'Lessons From Venezuela'** Simon Flowers from Wood Mackenzie. says that "Venezuela's slide from top of the heap to a virtual bit player in the oil market is a slow-motion car crash. Production sank progressively from 2.6m barrels per day (b/d) a decade ago, when it was third in Opec behind only Saudi Arabia and Iran, to 2m b/d by Q3 2017. Decline since has been precipitous – today it's just 1.1m b/d." A car crash that Guyana has to avoid at all costs.

Back to the UK and North Sea oil based in Aberdeen. Mark Lammey, Energy Editor of the *Aberdeen Press and Journal* in **'Lessons from Aberdeen'** says that Guyana can learn much from the experiences of the oil capital of the

UK and warns "Guyana should learn from this cautionary tale and make sure it thinks of ways in which its oil wealth can be put towards the development of a more rounded, resilient economy."

Bobby Gossai is a Guyanese studying for a PhD at, inevitably, the University of Aberdeen. In **'A blueprint for sustained success'** he finds that a disciplined stewardship of the windfall from Guyana's new petroleum finds could lead to great long-term prosperity. That means macro-economic action. Now.

He concludes: "One major imperative for Guyana is to focus on removing barriers to productivity across five key areas of the economy: the resources sector itself; resource rider sectors such as utilities and construction; manufacturing; local services such as retail trade and financial services; and agriculture."

Dr Frank Anthony. former Guyana Government Minister, is another wannabe President in waiting. In **'From Raleigh to Liza – the quest for riches'** he explores the future with a nod to the past. "As Raleigh had suspected all these years, Guyana has lots of riches, but in the end, you have to know where to look and how to manage it. Liza much like gold shines with the promise of hope to our people. However, it is still anybody's guess whether the black gold will be managed well enough to propel Guyana's prosperity through the 21st century."

Finally, the doyen of the oil economics trade in the Caribbean, Professor Anthony T Bryan of University of the West Indies, writes on **'Finding El Dorado? Oil and Gas Exploration in the Caribbean – the whole picture'**. In this he says: "A prosperous roadmap can be out in place for the whole region, but very careful management is the key. At present, the deep-water exploration in the Southern Caribbean and the 'Three Guianas' (Guyana French Guiana and Suriname) is not a recipe for hyperbole. Rather it is an opportunity for us to design the roadmaps for regional prosperity."

And we end as we begun this with a poetry salute to Guyana and Guyanese toil by Grace Nichols, half of the Guyanese poetry power couple, in **'Rainforest Interlude'**

My own love letter is complete; time to use that Guyanese passport and become part of the 'local content' to the nascent industry. Enjoy the book.

Chapter 1

Sir Walter Raleigh and El Dorado: the myth traced to source

For more than 500 years the quest for El Dorado, the mythical city of gold in South America has persisted. Nobody has ever found it – even the original explorer Sir Walter Raleigh. Christopher Minster explores the background

El Dorado, the legendary lost city of gold rumoured to be somewhere in the unexplored interior of South America, claimed many victims as thousands of Europeans braved flooded rivers, frosty highlands, endless plains and steamy jungles in the vain search for gold.

The most well-known of the obsessed men who searched for it, however, must be Sir Walter Raleigh, the legendary Elizabethan courtier who made two trips to South America to search for it.

The myth itself

There is a grain of truth in the El Dorado myth. The Muisca culture of Colombia had a tradition where their king would cover himself in gold dust and dive into Lake Guatavitá – Raleigh heard the story and began searching for the kingdom of El Dorado – 'the Gilded One'.

Lake Guatavita was dredged and some gold was found, but not very much, so the legend persisted. The supposed location of the lost city changed frequently as dozens of expeditions failed to find it. By 1580 or so the lost city of gold was thought to be in the mountains of present-day Guyana, a harsh and inaccessible place. The city of gold was referred to as El Dorado or Manoa, after a city told of by a Spaniard who had been captive of natives for ten years.

Sir Walter arrives

Sir Walter Raleigh was a member of the court of Queen Elizabeth I of England, whose favour he enjoyed. He was a true Renaissance man: he wrote history and poems, was a decorated sailor and dedicated explorer and settler. He fell out of favour with the Queen when he secretly married one of her maids in 1592: he was even imprisoned in the Tower of London for a time.

He talked his way out of the Tower, however, and convinced the Queen to allow him to mount an expedition to the New World to conquer El Dorado before the Spanish found it. Never one to miss the chance to out-do the Spanish, the Queen agreed to send Raleigh on his quest.

The capture of Trinidad

Raleigh and his brother Sir John Gilbert rounded up investors, soldiers, ships, and supplies. On 6 February, 1595 they set out from England with five small ships. His expedition was an act of open hostility to Spain, which jealously guarded its New World possessions.

They reached the Trinidad where they cautiously checked out the Spanish forces. The Englishmen attacked and captured the town of San Jose. They took an important prisoner on the raid: Antonio de Berrio, a high-ranking Spaniard who had spent years searching for El Dorado himself. Berrio told Raleigh what he knew about Manoa and El Dorado, trying to discourage the Englishman from continuing on his quest, but his warnings were in vain.

Raleigh left his ships anchored at Trinidad and took only 100 men to the mainland to begin his search. His plan was to go up the Orinoco River to the Caroni River and then follow it until he reached a legendary lake where he would find the city of Manoa. Raleigh had caught wind of a massive Spanish expedition to the area, so he was in a hurry to get underway.

He and his men headed up the Orinoco on a collection of rafts, ship's boats and even a modified galley. Although they were aided by natives who knew the river, the going was very tough as they had to fight the current of the mighty Orinoco River. The men, a collection of desperate sailors and cut-throats from England, were unruly and difficult to manage.

Topiawari

Laboriously Raleigh and his men made their way upriver. They found a friendly village, ruled by an aged chieftain named Topiawari. As he had been doing since arriving on the continent, Raleigh made friends by announcing that he was an enemy of the Spanish, who were widely detested by the natives. Topiawari told Raleigh of a rich culture living in the mountains. Raleigh easily convinced himself that the culture was an offshoot of the rich Inca culture of Peru and that it must be the fabled city of Manoa. The Spanish set out up the Caroni river, sending out scouts to look for gold and mines, all the while making friends with any natives they encountered. His scouts brought back rocks, hoping that further analysis would reveal gold ore.

Although Raleigh thought he was close, he decided to turn around. The rains were increasing, making the rivers even more treacherous, and he also feared being caught by the rumoured Spanish expedition. He felt he had enough evidence with his rock samples to drum up enthusiasm back in England for a return venture. He made an alliance with Topiawari, promising mutual aid when he returned. The English would help fight the Spanish, and the natives would help Raleigh find and conquer Manoa. As part of the deal, Raleigh left two men behind and took Topiawari's son back to England. The return journey was much easier, as they were traveling downstream: the Englishmen were joyful at seeing their ships still anchored off of Trinidad.

Return to England

Raleigh paused on his way back to England for a bit of privateering, attacking the island of Margarita and then the port of Cumaná, where he dropped off Berrio, who had remained a prisoner on board Raleigh's ships while he looked for Manoa. He returned to England in August of 1595 and was disappointed to learn that news of his expedition had preceded him and that it was already considered a failure.

Queen Elizabeth had little interest in the rocks he had brought back. His enemies seized upon his journey as an opportunity to slander him, claiming that the rocks were either fake or worthless. Raleigh defended himself ably, but was surprised to find very little enthusiasm for a return trip in his home country.

Legacy of Raleigh's first search for El Dorado

Raleigh would get his return trip to Guiana, but not until 1617: more than 20 years later. This second journey was a complete failure and directly led to Raleigh's execution back in England.

In between, Raleigh financed and supported other English expeditions to Guyana, which brought him more 'proof', but the search for El Dorado was becoming a hard sell.

In 1617, he returned to the New World on a second expedition, this time with Lawrence Kemys and his son, Watt Raleigh, to continue his quest for El Dorado. However, Raleigh, by now an old man, stayed behind in a camp on the island of Trinidad. Watt Raleigh was killed in a battle with Spaniards and Kemys subsequently committed suicide. Upon Raleigh's return to England, King James ordered him to be beheaded for disobeying orders to avoid conflict with the Spanish. He was executed in 1618.

Raleigh's greatest accomplishment may have been in creating good relations between the English and the natives of South America. Although Topiawari passed away not long after Raleigh's first voyage, the goodwill remained and future English explorers benefitted from it.

Today, Sir Walter Raleigh is remembered for many things, including his writings and his participation in the 1596 attack on the Spanish port of Cadiz, but he will forever be associated with the vain quest for El Dorado.

Source

Silverberg, Robert. *The Golden Dream: Seekers of El Dorado. Athens: the Ohio University Press, 1985*

About the contributor

Christopher Minster is a Professor at the Universiad San Francisco de Quito in Equador. He is a specialist in Latin American literature and history with a PhD in Spanish from Ohio State University.

Chapter 2

The oil *baccoo* takes up residence

Indranie Deolall recalls a cautionary Guyanese folktale in which fragile receptacles, waiting to be freed by the unsuspecting, conceal dangerous abilities and unquenchable appetites. Is this a warning for the years ahead?

As a child I loved accompanying my stout father, *Mr Big*, to the city sea wall for his regular swim after a brisk walk atop the crumbling 'Fort Groyne'. Built near the strategic site of a former British garrison that watched over the coveted sliver of low-lying coastline and the adjoining mouth of the Demerara River, the concrete erosion barrier jutted out into the ocean like a fat index finger, at the far end of breezy Kingston.

It was here, in 1781, British Lieutenant Colonel Robert Kingston decided to establish the little settlement that would become the capital Georgetown, after capturing the Dutch colony of Demerara-Essequibo and moving the administrative centre from Borselen Island far up the murky waterway.

While Dad waded out past the squelchy flats, to exercise in the deeper waters discoloured grey-brown by Amazonian mud, I danced barefoot on the warm beach, and screamed and squinted at him, a mere dot, bouncing up and down in the waves.

Racing in the surf, hair streaming, the sharp taste of salt in my mouth, I would search for signs of that history, specimens and sea glass gems smoothened by the frothing Atlantic that has witnessed centuries of conflict and ships ferrying foreign explorers forever fixed on finding fame and fortune.

One evening, intrigued by the Portuguese man-o-war that drifted in with the currents, I bent to pick up the purple and blue blob, when my family, who had accompanied us, screamed at me in a chorus to drop it. Instead, I collected the tiny coloured bottles scattered among the detritus, as the light faded. But these were all hurled away by my strangely angry mother. I learnt, to my chagrin and shock, that like 'the floating terror', no corked glass container, regardless of how pretty the hue, was to be even touched, and God forbid, retained and opened.

Our cautionary folktales, such as those she related that night, warn of the temperamental forces that supposedly lie trapped in fragile receptacles waiting to be freed by the unsuspecting, their size concealing dangerous abilities and unquenchable appetites.

The origins of *baccoo*

Of West African origin, according to the late Guyanese linguist and lexicographer, Dr Richard Allsopp, the word *baccoo* stems from ba-ku meaning death/corpse and led to the Saramaccan bakulu, a dwarf-spirit.

The *baccoo* is "an active, wicked spirit believed to take the form of some small, living, partly human being that must be kept in a bottle and may be commanded either to bring its owner great wealth or to do harm to other persons," explained the Creole expert in his *Dictionary of Caribbean English Usage*.

With an unexplained lust for the plump bacuba or red-skinned bananas belonging to the Cavendish group, and fresh milk, the creature often misbehaves by abruptly moving items, pelting homes with rocks and causing general mayhem.

Suspicious displays of excess gold and sudden riches are put down to a well-fed *baccoo* but since they tend to be mischievous, intelligent and deceitful, the infernal beings shapeshift, tormenting and destroying their owners when the mood, madness and hunger strike.

These days, besides the usual abundant catch of prawns and fish, local seas are finally yielding deep-down troves of treasures tens of millions of years old, that could bring unimagined wealth to an unprepared nation, one of the most impoverished in the hemisphere.

The oil *baccoo* is out. *Mr Big*, in this case, is the savvy pack leader, the Texas-based giant ExxonMobil (XOM), among the world's largest publicly traded international energy companies, which is pinning its hopes on Guyana for a revival.

The firm's astonishing exploration success in just the last few years has made the Guyana basin an exciting 'Oil Dorado', pulling the most prominent firms in the industry to snap up prime acreage. In May 2015, the XOM-led consortium announced its first 'significant' find after a decades-long search with the Liza-1 well in the lucrative and huge 6.6m acre Stabroek Block yielding high-quality oil-bearing sandstone reservoirs, about 120 miles offshore. Crude prices were plummeting at the time, sinking to a 12-year low of about $26 (all figures in US dollars) a barrel in 2016.

Foreign ownership

ExxonMobil's Esso Exploration and Production Guyana Ltd holds a 45 per cent stake in the block. The subsidiary of another major American corporation, Hess Guyana Exploration controls 30 per cent. China's National Offshore Oil Corporation (CNOOC), which, this January, closed its milestone $15.1bn acquisition of Canadian Nexen owns 25 per cent, through its rebranded CNOOC International division.

Since then, the discoveries keep coming. Just this year, XOM announced its 11th and 12th major oil and gas finds in the south-eastern section, Tilapia-1 and Haimara-1, bearing the common names of local fishes, and taking its Guyana estimated recoverable resources to more than five billion barrels of oil equivalent.

With the country's first oil well expected to produce up to 120,000 barrels per day by early 2020, and at least another dozen or so likely, some analysts predict production could exceed a million barrels daily over the next decade, rocketing this small country from a nobody to a newfound star shining in non-Opec's (the Organisation of Petroleum Exporting Countries) top ten. A mere two of the wildcat wells have missed, representing a phenomenal success rate of more than 80 per cent.

Given its population of about 800,000, a large diaspora and a meagre Gross Domestic Product (GDP) per capita of just over $4,000, Guyana stands on the brink of unprecedented riches.

However, it will need to set aside long simmering ethnic mistrust and endless political bickering, heightened by the recent surprise passage of a divisive no confidence motion in the Government, and get its act together before the non-renewable oil runs outs. Avoiding the resource curse that so visibly haunts states like oil bulwark Venezuela, imploding next door, and aggressively renewing claims to three quarters of Guyana, will mean disciplined investing in a substantial sovereign wealth fund.

Even with the low two per cent royalty on gross earnings and 50 per cent of oil proceeds, at the current average market price of $50 per barrel, Guyana can expect to earn $1m a day.

Realms of gold

Simon Flowers (who also writes chapter 11 of this book), chairman and chief analyst of respected Scotland-based global resources research and consultancy group Wood Mackenzie, spoke of his sense of wonder over Guyana. Rephrasing the famous lines of Romantic poet John Keats' *On First Looking into Chapman's Homer*, he posted, "I felt like some watcher of the skies when a new planet swims into his ken." Incidentally, the poem starts with the phrase, "Much have I travell'd in the realms of gold..."

"The discovery of a major new oil player like Guyana instils the same sense of wonder on we oil industry devotees," Flowers acknowledged in an online piece last September. "Few oil-producing countries produce more than one million barrels per day. Outside of Opec you can count them on two hands: Canada, USA and Mexico; UK and Norway; China, Brazil and Oman; Russia and most recently Kazakhstan – the only new member in the 21st century. New admissions to the group don't happen very often," Flowers said. "Guyana, with no upstream oil industry four years ago, has a very good chance of joining this elite group."

In a February 2019 commentary on what Guyana can learn from the Venezuelan crisis, he warned against the temptation "to spend, spend, spend." Opposing dependence on a single source of revenue, Flowers singled out infrastructure building and raising education standards to help develop other sectors.

"Our analysis of the upstream project assumes total investment of over $30bn; plateauing at $5bn annually in the early 2020s as the known discoveries are developed; all perhaps matched by investment down the value chain onshore. Tax revenues kick in from the mid-2020s and build up quickly to more than $10bn per annum."

Flowers pointed out, "For such a small economy, the scale of development is staggering. Assuming oil production of one million barrels daily by 2030, Guyana's output per person will be higher than any other major oil producer. A four-fold increase in the size of its economy over a decade is possible, catapulting Guyana into the high-income bracket."

"It will be a delicate balancing act. The role of government is also central to success in setting clear energy policy, establishing firm and independent regulation, and a stable fiscal policy. These set a framework for close collaboration with international operators. The fate of Venezuela is all the incentive needed to get this right," he stressed.

A fairy tale

Exxon's Senior Vice President Neil Chapman, a management-board member, compared the Guyana developments to the magic of a 'fairy tale' at the company's analysts' day in March 2018. According to the 2012 World Petroleum Resources Project by the United States Geological Survey, the assessed provinces of the region including South America and the Caribbean have a mean estimate of 126bn barrels of oil in offshore reservoirs. The Guyana–Suriname Basin has at least 12bn barrels.

As the *baccoos* remind us, it is painfully ironic that the very resources slated to bring Guyana unexpected wealth will also contribute to increasing vulnerability. Most experts agree the burning of non-renewable fossil fuels such as oil and natural gas releases carbon dioxide into the atmosphere, thickening the layers of greenhouse gases and making the Earth warmer.

This could mean a rather grim future for low-lying and impoverished countries like Guyana, with the bulk of the population and industries confined to a fragile and narrow strip of coastland. Residents already struggle with the regular consequences of floods with each black sky and heavy rainfall, rising sea levels and weather shifts. The worst-case context would mean eventually relocating the entire belt to higher zones further inland.

Declining to hear oil giant ExxonMobil's appeal in its suit with the state of Massachusetts, the United States Supreme Court in January issued an important ruling for ongoing legal battles around climate change.

In the appeal XOM tried to block the release of incriminating records that it knew burning fossil fuels alters the climate. Massachusetts Attorney General Maura Healey filed the suit against the giant in 2016 alleging that it violated state consumer protection rules and misled investors about the impact of fossil fuels on climate change, and the ensuing business risks, media reports indicated.

American journalist Steve Coll describes an illuminating exchange in 2001 between then President George W Bush and the Indian Prime Minister Atal Bihari Vajpayee. Worried that ExxonMobil was delaying a deal with India's largest state-owned oil company, Vajpayee allegedly asked Bush: "Why don't you just tell them what to do?" The 43rd President's response was ominous: "Nobody tells those guys what to do!" Much like the rampaging Guyanese *baccoos*.

About the contributor

Indranie Deolall is a Guyanese-born journalist based in Trinidad. She is a columnist for the private newspaper, *Stabroek News*.

Chapter 3

The possible thoughts of Wilson Harris

What would one of Guyana's greatest writers have made of black gold?
Michael Mitchell has some answers

"Guiana is a country that hath yet her maidenhead..." wrote Sir Walter Raleigh in the account of his expedition: The Discovery of the Large, Rich and Beautiful Empire of Guiana, with a relation of the Great and Golden City of Manoa (Which the Spaniards call El Dorado), published in Hakluyt's The Principal Navigation, Voyages, Traffics, and Discoveries of the English Nation (1598-1600).[1]

Raleigh dreamed of penetrating it, but his account was a dream of Trumpian bombast, and all his expeditions to the South American coast resulted in was the loss of his head. There is a long history to the vain search for material wealth in Guiana, from gold to sugar and now oil.

In his earliest published novel, Palace of the Peacock, Wilson Harris summons the myth of El Dorado by making it a journey into the interior. It was assumed that El Dorado, golden man or golden lake or golden city, if it existed at all outside of legend, must be somewhere in the barely accessible rainforest or in the heartlands of Guyana, where it meets the vast Amazon basin.

So Harris, in describing a journey upriver towards a waterfall much like Kaieteur, seems to be alluding to that myth. He called on his own experiences leading a surveying team up the rivers on behalf of the colonial government anxious to explore the possibilities of harnessing the waters for hydro-electric power. Of course, there was indeed gold in the Guyanese interior, but in such small quantities it hardly sustained the efforts of the isolated pork-knockers who panned the rivers for it, and the terrain proved unsuitable for hydro-electric schemes.

In fact, Palace of the Peacock does not mention El Dorado explicitly at all, but in his introduction (1984) to the Guyana Quartet he refers to the men who go up the river as an 'Eldoradonne crew'. They are led by Donne, a name consciously chosen by Harris alluding to John Donne, the metaphysical poet. Donne embodies both the man of action, driving his crew to enslave the 'folk' to work his estates in the savannahs beyond the rainforest, but at the same time the reflective narrator, a kind of twin. The one is a figure in pursuit of material wealth, the other is questioning what that wealth really means and what it might cost.

The journey becomes a quest on the part of a crew who are already dead, but are unaware of the fact, ostensibly for riches and the exploitation of both the human and natural world, but who are confronted in their second death with the possibility of gaining alchemical rather than material gold.

An allegory of alchemical processes

The whole novel can be seen as an allegory of alchemical processes. As Harris puts it in his 'Note on the Genesis of The Guyana Quartet' (1985), the distances they travel into the interior "breed a gateway or intangible architecture when El Dorado, or the city of gold, secretes a resemblance to the City of God".[2] The key to unlock this mystery is introduced at the beginning of the novel: "I dreamt I awoke with one dead seeing eye and one living closed eye."[3]

We may recall Blake's appeal to the visionary experience: "May God us keep from Single vision and Newton's sleep!"[4] For Blake, Newton represented a world bounded by material, in which wealth is bound up with exploitation and 'satanic mills'. Harris, likewise, was well aware of the cost, in human and environmental terms, of the search for easy wealth.

Towards the end of his extraordinary career Harris returns to this theme in his essay Theatre of the Arts (2002). Harris considers the nature of boundaries which appear fixed, like that between human beings and apparently inanimate nature, which only appears to resist human exploitation in major convulsions or the slow catastrophes we now begin to observe across the planet. We do not understand, in other words, that our culture's 'single vision' fails to perceive what is actually true:

"There is a measureless nature to the life of the earth in the midst of catastrophes, drought and famine and flood that we blindly invite, a precarious freedom we need to understand if our cultures are to awaken from their 'sleep' or 'obliviousness' which seems so strong it is called realism."[5]

The effects on conquered cultures

Our realism tends to see the cultures conquered by imperialism and the apparently lifeless landscape of the inanimate world as passive: "We have seized on such passivity with what seems an all-powerful technology, we have brushed aside ancient legends of gods of the wind and the sea and the earth and the air without a thought of their intuitive depth, their intuitive bridle on the horses of the earth — horses of wind and sea — that needed a greater re-creative understanding and development."[6]

In the essay, Harris quotes his 1968 novel Tumatumari as an attempt to portray a moving, living landscape. Through it he shows that what seemed fixed stages, the foundations of our cities, are instead 'sentient and alive'. The apparent strength with which our technology solves superficial difficulties and obliterates indigenous cultures contains a hidden infirmity, through which new ways of seeing become possible. Tumatumari is an Amerindian word meaning 'sleeping rocks'.

Harris says: "In the novel I sought to bring the 'sleep' of a traumatized people, traumatised by conquest, into league with sculptures that have sprung from the earth — sculptured crests, sculptured outlines, sculptured exposures — in order to engage in an awakening, within many-sided nature, from the brutalisation of every-day place and person by conquistadorial legacies."[7]

In the discussion which followed a reading of this paper in 2001 at the British Braids Conference at Brunel University, Harris added: "But the Amerindians themselves have forgotten why they call it the sleeping rocks. They have been so conditioned by the traumatisations of conquest that they don't know why they call it the sleeping rocks. It is up to us to get into it, and see what sleeping rocks mean."[8]

Ways to heal

Harris is insistent that we must find ways — through the arts, he would argue — to discover and heal the infirmity within our conquistadorial behaviour, not only towards cultures but also towards the natural world.

At the end of his late novel about the conquest of Peru, The Dark Jester, Harris juxtaposes what he calls Cartesian form (the basis of our realism), personified in Pizarro, the conqueror, with Atahualpan form, which he conceives as a sort of Trojan Horse in reverse, allowing access through a wound to a different vision, in which the plunder of Inca treasures ceases to be a desired goal. He speaks in the voice of the last Inca Emperor:

> *I dream I am Tupac Amaru in world theatre.*
>
> *I cross to Vilcabamba. My pursuers follow and find nothing but a smoking ruin like mist above water. I am there. Yet I have left for the Amazon. I seek El Dorado. It is precious to me as much as Troy was to King Priam and Cassandra.*
>
> *This is the City of Cities, El Dorado. I bring to it the ruins of the past, the memory of places I know as mine but which are taken by Europe and Spain. El Dorado is the Troy of the Americas.*[9]

Tupac Amaru, though, is captured, and his vision of El Dorado is lost: "El Dorado hides on a saddle of ground on a Misty Animal in the Amazon [...] El Dorado vanishes. It is swallowed in the belly of a gigantic Horse or Animal of space. [...] Will it give birth — some day in the future — to avengers or to compassions?"[10] On the scaffold Tupac Amaru can see: "The land that is mine has become desolate."[11] Harris's art is to show the relationship of the gold to the desolation, and a hidden ship with a flimsy sail to find, like Odysseus, the way Home.

Wilson Harris did not live to see the full proposals for the exploitation of the oil reserves, the black gold, beneath Guyana's coastlines, but the notes above suggest, I think, how he might have reacted to the news.

Notes

1. Quoted in Gianluca Delfino, *Time, History and Philosophy in the Works of Wilson Harris* (Stuttgart: ibidem-Verlag, 2012), p. 127
2. Wilson Harris, *The Guyana Quartet* (London: Faber and Faber, 1985), p. 8.
3. ibid., p. 19.
4. William Blake, *Complete Writings*, ed. Geoffrey Keynes (Oxford: Oxford UP, 1969), p. 818.
5. Wilson Harris, 'Theatre of the Arts', in Hena Maes-Jelinek and Bénédicte Ledent (eds.), *Theatre of the Arts: Wilson Harris and the Caribbean* (Amsterdam & New York: Rodopi, 2002), p. 3 (author's emphases).
6. ibid. p. 4 (author's emphases)
7. ibid. p. 4.

8. https://www.brunel.ac.uk/creative-writing/research/entertext/documents/entertext021/Wilson-Harris-Theatre-of-the-Arts.pdf
9. Wilson Harris, *The Dark Jester* (London: Faber and Faber, 2001), pp. 106f.
10. ibid., p. 108.
11. ibid., p. 109.

About the contributor

Dr Michael Mitchell is an honorary visiting professor at the Yesu Persaud Centre for Caribbean Studies, University of Warwick. He is the author of *Hidden Mutualities: Faustian Themes from Gnostic Origins to the Postcolonial* (Rodopi, 2006) and has written extensively on the Caribbean, particularly on Wilson Harris. He has also written a number of school textbooks for students of English in Germany, where he now teaches.

Chapter 4

Guyana's oil discoveries to date

Just how much oil is there? Sally Gibson of Petro Legal, Guyanese by birth, and John Mair outline the progress of the search for the new black gold in just one field

'Every Man, Woman and Child in British Guiana Must Become Oil-Minded!'

British Guiana Daily Chronicle 1932

Some 87 years later after that pronouncement, Guyana has become an emerging oil nation with world class petroleum discoveries of at least five billion barrels.

Considerable exploration activity has taken place in Guyana since the 1970s with 22 wells drilled: no commercial discoveries were then found. The Lisa development was discovered in the Stabroek Block in 2015 by ExxonMobil (EXM) and its current partners, Hess and CNOOC Nexen. The Stabroek Block, which covers some 6.6m acres was first licenced to EXM and Shell in 1999.

The Lisa discovery is located some 120 miles off the coast of Guyana in deep water. Four wells have been drilled on Lisa confirming petroleum reserves in excess of one billion barrels. The Lisa 3 well identified a deeper reservoir directly below the Lisa Field. EXM and partners have drilled 12 exploration wells to date, two of which have been dry holes (Skipjack and Sorubim). This represents a success rate of 82 per cent, which is staggering since the industry average worldwide is around 20 per cent. EXM and partners have so far made 12 discoveries, each in 12 separate reservoirs.

DISCOVERY	NAME	EST. BARRELS OF OIL
1	Lisa	Excess of one billion
2	Lisa 3 Deep	100-150m
3	Payara	500m
4	Snoek	Not published
5	Turbot	Not published
6	Ranger	346m
7	Pacora	Not published
8	Longtail	Not published
9	Hammerhead	Not published
10	Pluma	300m
11	Tilapia-1	Not published
12	Haimara-1	Not published
	TOTAL	**5 bn barrels minimum**

It is said that EXM and partners have identified another 19 targets to drill.

When will oil come on stream?

First oil from Liza phase 1 is expected in 2020, with peak production rates of 120,000 barrels per day. Liza phase 2 is expected to produce 220,000 barrels per day. The nearby Payara development has first oil planned for 2023. The oil will be produced from five floating production storage offloading vessels (FPSOs). It is estimated that Guyana could be producing 750,000 barrels per day by 2025.

In 2016, following the year of discovery, the oil price had hit a low of $25 per barrel. The oil price is currently around $60 per barrel The breakeven price for the Lisa discovery is said to be below $40 per barrel.

Is that the end?

In 2012, the United States Geological Survey estimated that that there was 13.6bn barrels of oil and 32 trillion cubic feet of natural gas yet to be discovered in the Guyana-Suriname basin. Others are exploring other areas offshore of Guyana with much anticipated success.

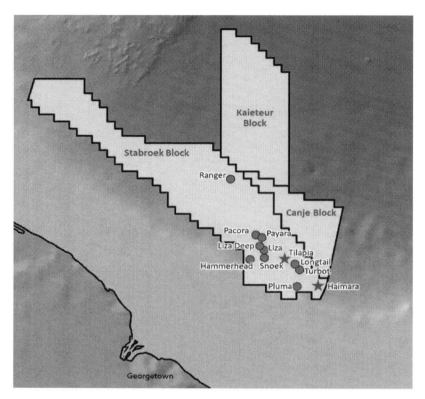

Source ExxonMobil

About the contributor

Sally Gibson a qualified barrister, is a highly regarded international energy lawyer with more than 38 years' experience of the oil and gas sector. During her early career Sally worked for a number of international oil companies before forming her own independent energy consultancy, Petro-Legal Limited, which she has managed successfully for the last 24 years. She has worked with private and state-owned companies and negotiated contracts with host governments as well as international oil companies.

Chapter 5

A nation with ambition at its heart

In the next decade Guyana will be producing one barrel of oil per person per day. Charles Cosad reports on how developing an oilfield industry for the benefit of all is no small task

The world will be watching, since Guyana is the first country to discover its first oil in the age of the Internet. The oil discoveries offshore the country by ExxonMobil in the Stabroek block are among the largest finds in a generation. With it, Guyana is in a unique position – the country has an opportunity to show the world how to develop a sustainable energy industry. It has made a promising start.

In a landscape of beautiful nature, and still with many dirt roads and clapboard towns, Guyana, with its population of approximately 760,000 seems an unlikely place to be pinned as the Oman of Latin America. Guyana's 2017 GDP of $3.6bn (all figures in US dollars) ranks the country 161st out of 193 surveyed countries[2].

Economists predict the oil discovery will triple the country's current GDP in as little as five years[3]. The implications of such an injection of liquidity for Guyana cannot be overstated. As defined by social scientist Daron Acemoglu in his influential book *Why Nations Fail*, Guyana is a 'critical juncture' in its history. He defines this as a point at which decisions made today will result in either long term gain and prosperity for all, which he refers to as inclusivity, or a wasted opportunity with corruption, benefiting a limited few, referred to as exclustivity[4].

Guyana has had opportunities to develop 'inclusivity' in the past through mining and sugar industries – without good success. The oil discovery may well be this country's last chance; it is "...providence," said Raphael Trotman, the natural resources minister. "We've been given a second chance to get things right."[5]

Getting started

How best to answer this multi-billion dollar question? How best to capture the long-term economic value for the Guyanese people? "The challenges are enormous and shouldn't be underestimated," said Lars Mangal, CEO of TOTALTEC Oilfield Services, a Guyanese company that trains local workers in safety and basic oil operations and forms partnerships with international companies. "We have to overcome nepotism, entitlements, corruption, cynicism and scepticism," he said.

Mangal continued, "People, partnerships and facilities. These are the pillars necessary as local companies form and adapt to take part in the new Guyana oil industry. People will require entirely new skills, from the most basic hands on roles, where safety is critical, to highly technical engineering and geoscience ones."

"Partnerships with international companies will allow local ones to accelerate their ability to take ownership of an ever increasing workscope of their new industry. The oilfield has unique facilities requirements, from onshore supply bases, service company bases, machine shops, and the like, to offices which enable companies to operate to international standards."

People – what really counts

It is useful to consider two groups of people; first there are those who can immediately go to work in any number of positions following some basic, conversion training. Second are those in school programs, where new curricula must be developed or attend international higher education in oilfield related programs.

Many Guyanese have gone to work in the service industry in entry level positions, a good start. One of the most visible initial metrics of local content has been 'percent Guyanese headcount' in a given company.

A number of international service companies have published these percentages and are to be commended. These percentages may look significant but are unfortunately what the business world call a vanity metric; these positions require limited skills, with limited opportunity for advancement.

It is easy for international companies to pause on this initial plateau. The metric may read 50 per cent or more, but it is not meaningful in the long term. It is getting from 50 to 60 and beyond with skilled and responsible positions that really counts.

The Guyanese Government and local oilfield service companies are now working with international organisations to establish development plans and metrics for advancing Guyanese people.

Many Guyanese have highly relevant skills and experience from the mining and sugar industries. Guyana also has an active maritime industry, with many mechanics, electricians and technically trained operators. They are ready to take on more senior roles after an initial cross-training and experience period. There are examples with international service companies where this has already occurred, a very positive first step.

Given opportunity and training, engineers and other technical people can readily move into equivalent positions to the industry they come from. That training may come from spending time outside Guyana. Said Mangal, "Consider a government policy where if a company has several professional, expatriate staff working in Guyana operations, a similar number of Guyanese must be outside the country in those positions, training, with plans to return."

A number of Guyanese are off to a good start following training given locally to international standards, for example at the International Petroleum and Maritime Academy (IPMA), the Marine Safety Training Institute (MSTI), and Matpal Marine Institute.

In the longer term, with the support of international companies, Guyanese schools, technical academies and universities will begin to produce graduates who will be the workforce of the future. ExxonMobil has taken a leading role in supporting these institutions, showing the way forward for other operating companies who are already coming in to explore, and will likely have success.

The Guyanese and international oilfield service companies must be ready to put these new graduates to work, on progressive career paths that end in Guyanese people leading their new industry.

Partnerships, balancing business and society

The second pillar depends on developing transparent partnerships with international service companies and entities outside Guyana with the skills, assets and experience the country does not currently possess.

The partnerships must be inclusive and working for the long term benefit of the country. Objectives must be set and regularly reviewed. Beyond the initial headcount advances, international service companies will need to be pushed through government guidance and metrics for impactful partnerships. Partnerships strategically developed today will bring Guyanese the skills and experience required to lead the oil and gas industry in the future.

A metric relevant to partnerships is the percent of total oilfield services and products spend with local Guyanese companies. The time to start measuring this is now; although the proportion is certainly very low today. Government institutions will be required to drive local content in oilfield service and product provision, working alongside international companies.

Much of the equipment used in the provision of oilfield services is commercially available. In the near term, a majority of onshore services in Guyana can be delivered by local companies. This is well underway with examples of the Guyana Shore Base, Inc. (GYSBI) and Jaguar Oilfield Services. A fair amount of offshore services can be performed with commercially available equipment, and this needs to be driven. Offshore services and the metrics around delivery is the ultimate goal of Guyanese businesses. Their ability to compete in and serve the offshore industry will determine their ultimate success.

There have been a number of international service companies that have made excellent initial steps in forming partnerships and growing local content; for example Noble, Saipem, SBM, Schlumberger, Stena Drilling and TechnipFMC. They are to be commended and are the logical starting points for the next step of services and products provision.

Facilities – raising the bar across the country

The final pillar critical to Guyana growing its own oilfield companies is facilities. The oilfield has unique facilities requirements. These range from supply bases to handle large volumes of equipment and speciality fluids, to speciality machining and equipment testing facilities.

The development of a country's infrastructure complements this critical need and requires transparency and accountability at the highest levels of government. The Guyanese Government is taking the right steps towards creating these inclusive institutions.

The newly created Department of Energy (DoE), headed by Mark Bynoe and empowered to regulate the oil and gas industry, is one such move. The long-term vision of the DoE is to become a ministry with a wider remit, developing and furthering energy infrastructure for both hydrocarbons and renewable sources across the country, to the benefit of all people. This is a strong vision, and the right one for Guyana.

The road ahead (...or is it pipeline?)

A healthy mix of local and international oil and service companies are working together to put in place the necessary foundation for a Guyanese-led, inclusive oil and gas industry. It is early times and will be helped by government putting in place guidance and metrics to drive it. Things are off to a good start.

When an updated version of *Why Nations Fail* is published, we believe Guyana will feature as an exceptional example of how it took the right steps to form inclusive institutions at its critical juncture, building an oil and gas industry beneficial to all.

Notes

1. https://www.gfmag.com/global-data/country-data/guyana-gdp-country-report [21st February 2019, 16:54 GMT]
2. https://countryeconomy.com/gdp/guyana [21st February 2019, 17:05 GMT]
3. https://www.nytimes.com/2018/07/20/business/energy-environment/the-20-billion-question-for-guyana.html [21st February, 16:03 GMT]
4. https://notesonliberty.com/2013/06/20/critical-junctures-and-path-dependency-in-why-nations-fail-implications-for-u-s-foreign-aid-policy/ [19th December 2018]
5. https://www.nytimes.com/2018/07/20/business/energy-environment/the-20-billion-question-for-guyana.html [21st February, 16:03 GMT]

Author's note

An online search of 'Guyana oil discoveries' will quickly find links to ExxonMobil and multiple other industry players and publications. It is the discovery of a generation. Within a decade, production will be one barrel of oil per Guyanese per day (yes, per day). TOTALTEC Oilfield Services is a local Guyanese company whose purpose is to make Guyana an exceptional example of what the discovery of oil can do for a people and a country, supporting partner companies to deliver to their highest performance standards.

About the contributor

Following a 38-year international career with Schlumberger, **Charles Cosad** advises oil and gas industry companies on marketing and business strategy, with a particular passion for the work of TOTALTEC Oilfield Services in supporting the development of oil for the benefit of Guyana, its society, and to serve as an example for the world of how to implement an 'all of the above energy strategy' to protect our challenged planet.

.

Chapter 6

A new age dawns, finally

The clues were there but it has taken decades of hope – and border disputes – for oil to be finally realised, says Christopher Ram

A quest that began in earnest some 170 years ago will soon become reality as Guyana – often the forgotten former British colony in South America – is set to become a top oil and gas producer on a per capita basis in just one year. Between May 2015 to January 2019, ExxonMobil, the American oil giant announced 12 'high impact discoveries of oil and gas' with estimated gross recoverable resource of between four and five billion oil-equivalent barrels.

In 1929 there was a banner headline in one of the colony's newspapers which screamed *'Every Man, Woman and Child Must Become Oil-Minded!'* Long before that, indications of Guyana's offshore oil capabilities came from reports of the early Dutch explorers who noted the occurrence of flotsam pitch. while in 1917 a person described in all the records only as J. Harrison discovered a thin deposit of heavy oil (pitch) near Krunkenae Point, on the west coast of the Waini River, in Region 1.[1] Following those earlier surface oil indications, the first hole was drilled at a site northwest of the Waini Mouth at the top of Guyana.

While a few drops of heavy oil were observed, the thickness of sediments was found inadequate for the formation of oil. Later wells drilled for water encountered seepages of gas, the most significant of which took place at Bath Estate on the bank of the Berbice River, which for many years was used for cooking purposes.

In 1939, 11 years after British Guiana had become a Crown colony[2], its new Legislative Council passed the Petroleum Production Act providing for the vesting in the Crown the property in petroleum and natural gas and making provision for the issue of separate licences for prospecting and exploration.

One year earlier, Trinidad Leaseholds Co. Ltd had been granted the first oil prospecting licence but abandoned it in 1942.[3]

In 1958, a one-month offshore marine reconnaissance seismic survey was carried out by subsidiaries of Standard Oil of California, and this was followed by several aeromagnetic surveys conducted between 1956 and 1965 traversing the onshore Takutu Basin[4]. Intrigued by the 1965 survey, Phoenix Oil Co of Canada showed interest in the Takutu Basin, and was granted acreage in 1966, but which it never took up.[5]

Decades of hope

In the five decades from the 1960s and up to the first decade of the 21st century, at least 20 companies principally from the USA, Canada and France, of which the most prominent were Shell Conoco/Tenneco, Home Oil and Mobil, made trial investigations. Additionally, there were organisations like the UNDP, World Bank and CIDA, which financed various studies in the search for oil. The most encouraging phase of activity in Guyana was clearly in the Takutu Basin located in the south western part of the country.

A significant activity to note within that time period is Home Oil of Canada, which drilled two wells in 1981 and 1982, of which the second well, Karanambo-1, produced 400 barrels of oil per day, apparently from fractured Apoteri Volcanics.[6] Despite this result, Home Oil eventually abandoned the well due to failure in acquiring additional partners to finance further drilling.

In the last ten years of the last century, a few others oil companies had sought and subsequently obtained prospecting and exploration licenses in Guyana. At present Nabi Oil and Gas, ON Energy, Tullow, Repsol, CGX Resources, Eco Atlantic Oil and Gas, Mid Atlantic Guyana, Esso & JHI Associates, CNOOC Nexen and Hess, Anadarko, Ratio Energy/Ratio Guyana and, of course, ExxonMobil, all have licences or are in partnership with a license holder to prospect and explore.

Figure 1: Licence holders with estimated hectares

Location	Block	Estimated Hectares	Licencee	Joint Venture Partner
Inland	Takutu Basin	1,000,000	Nil	Nil
Coastal	Mahaicony	260,000	Nabi Oil & Gas Inc.	Nil
	Berbice	333,000	ON Energy	Nil
Shelf	Kanuku	660,000	Repsol	Tullow
	Corentyne	630,000	CGX Resources Inc.	Nil
	Orinduik	180,000	Tullow	Eco Atlantic Oil and Gas
Deep-water	Canje	611,000	Mid Atlantic Guyana Inc.	Esso & JHI Associates
	Stabroek	2,700,000	Esso	CNOOC Nexen and Hess
Ultra Deep-water	Roraima	1,990,000	Anadarko	Nil
	Kaieteur	1,360,000	Ratio Energy Inc / Ratio Guyana Inc	Esso

Figure 2: Location of the offshore petroleum blocks

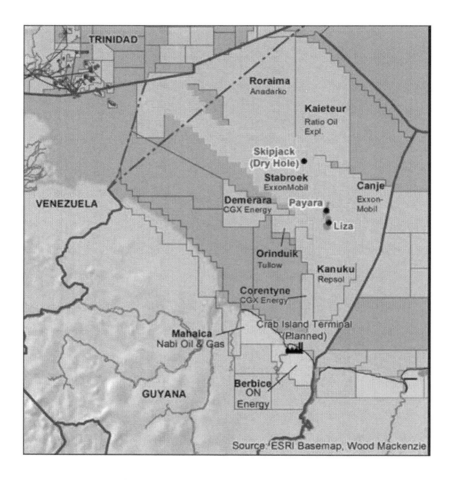

However, in its quest for oil, Guyana was hampered by the strong arm tactics of two of its neighbours – Suriname and Venezuela.

Guyana-Venezuela border controversy

Guyana's and Venezuela's strained relations have their origin in the colonisation of the Americas by competing European powers during an era when boundaries were not properly defined. A more formal approach to border-setting began in 1841 when Venezuela submitted to Great Britain a formal proposal for a boundary between it and the then British Guiana.

Britain showed little urgency in addressing the matter even after receiving a 10,000-words dispatch[7] from Richard Olney, then Secretary of State of the United States, demanding from the British a decision on whether it would submit the question to impartial arbitration. The response was dismissive and caused President Cleveland to be as 'mad clean through' when he read the reply.

Good sense later prevailed, and in 1897, an arbitral tribunal was established to determine the boundary between the two countries. It was agreed among the parties that *'the result of the proceeds of the tribunal of arbitration would constitute a full, perfect and final settlement of all the questions referred to the arbitrators'.*

The decision of the tribunal of 1899 was unanimous and was given effect to by a joint Venezuelan/British Mixed Boundary Commission in a demarcation exercise in 1901-1905. Thereafter, the story became wrapped up in international intrigue, accusations of bribery and alleged collusion by the British and American governments to keep out a left-leaning government in British Guiana, prior to independence from Britain. That led to what is referred to as the Geneva Agreement of 1966 agreed between the UK and Venezuela to resolve the controversy over the frontier between Venezuela and British Guiana.

Despite the agreement, Venezuela has remained steadfast in its claim, posing a great threat to Guyana's sovereignty and by extension its oil prospects. Following the announcement of the early discoveries, the Energy and Petroleum Commission of the National Assembly in Venezuela rejected the oil operations in the Essequibo region,[8] claiming that it violated the Geneva agreement of 1966 and Article 10 its constitution.[9] In fact, in 2015 the President of Venezuela issued a decree claiming the maritime area in which the oil exploration was being done, which he subsequently recalled.[10]

Legally, the fate of the controversy now rests with the International Court of Justice to which the matter has been taken by Guyana following the failure of a United Nations process. which saw the appointment of a good officer to resolve the controversy. Venezuela has refused to participate in the process. Practically, Guyana it seems is relying on the presence of a major American oil company in the controverted maritime territory as a protection of its rights.

Guyana-Suriname border dispute

The border dispute between Guyana and Suriname had its genesis in the 18th century, when colonial powers (Great Britain and Netherland) fought over land. In 1967, the Government of Suriname stated that in a treaty signed in 1799 between the Dutch and the British all of the territory west of the Corentyne river was ceded to the colony of Berbice and the border was the left bank of the Corentyne from its mouth to its source. The Suriname Government claimed that the Corentyne is a national river lying within its territory and not a boundary river.

Guyana's position was that the south-eastern boundary between Guyana and Suriname was determined by international agreement among the governments of Brazil, Great Britain and the Netherlands in 1936.

The concrete evidence of that agreement is the tri-junction point at the head of the Kutari River where their three territories touched. It took more than 150 years for a definitive resolution to permanently settle the correct boundary between Berbice and Suriname. This was achieved in 2007 after Guyana had initiated proceedings for a judicial settlement under the United Nations Convention on the Law of the Sea, to which both countries were signatories.

Notes

1. United Nations Technical Assistance Board, Reporting on the Prospecting for oil in British Guiana (United Nations: New York, 1965) 8-9.
2. M. Shahabudeen, Constitutional Development in Guyana 1621 – 1978 (Georgetown, Guyana Printers Ltd. 1978).
3. Exploration Consultants Ltd, Guyana Petroleum Exploration Appraisal, Guyana Basin, (Volume 1, 1985) 7-13.
4. UNDP reports 1965 and 1966.
5. Exploration Consultants Ltd, Guyana Petroleum Exploration Appraisal, Guyana Basin, (Volume 1, 1985) 7-13.
6. ibid
7. A dispatch made famous for the original articulation of the Monroe Doctrine in a written communication to a foreign government. See Cedric L. Joseph, Anglo-American Diplomacy and the Reopening of the Guyana – Venezuela Border Controversy, 1961 – 1966, at p 50.
8. Denis Chabrol, 'Venezuela says oil operations in Guyana violates agreement' Demerara Waves (Georgetown, March 17 2017)

<http://demerarawaves.com/2017/03/17/venezuela-says-oil-operations-in-guyana-violatesagreement/>
9. The Bolivarian Constitution of Venezuela, art 10
10. Denis Chabrol, 'Venezuela says oil operations in Guyana violates agreement' Demerara Waves (Georgetown, March 17 2017) http://demerarawaves.com/2017/03/17/venezuela-says-oil-operations-in-guyana-violatesagreement/

About the contributor

Christopher Ram is an attorney-at-law and chartered accountant with active practices in both fields. This chapter is an adaptation of a project paper submitted by the author under a 2017/2018 full-time distance learning programme for a Master of Laws in Oil and Gas Law at Reading University in the UK.

Chapter 7

Is Guyana ready for oil prime time?

The first oil is due March 2020 (or before) and then Guyana in the next five years will become one of largest oil producers in the world. Here former oil minister Robert Persaud looks both backwards and forwards

The initial – and long – history of looking for oil in Guyana

One of the riskiest of all businesses is oil and gas (O&G) exploration. The gamble climbs exponentially if it is taking place in a virgin basin, not yet proven its commercial potential. O&G projects are by nature risky ventures due to their complex nature, potentially environmental impact and high operational costs. This risks balloons for O&G exploration ventures in new frontiers. And then came Guyana.

Guyana's offshore, up until early 2015, was considered not only high-risk both un- and under-explored – but that was all to change.

First to be looked at was the Eagle 1 well, a 100 per cent undertaking by the Canadian business CGX which had received its petroleum agreement (PA) and petroleum prospecting licence (PPL). This well was estimated at 60 days of drilling, but due to weather and mechanical delays the drilling period had to be extended by another 30 days. The original budget was $55m (all figures in US dollars) but it went over by about $22m. The well encountered oil but not in a commercial quantity.

Second was the Jaguar 1 well – a consortium of Repsol, YPF Guyana, CGX and Tullow, which having received its PPL, launched the well drilling. This was to be the deepest well drilled in the Guyana-Suriname Basin at a projected depth of 6,500 metres over 180 days. Drilling started in February 2012 and by early July 2012, having reached 4,876 metres, operations had to be abandoned. The well was plugged without reaching its primary objective.

Then, in 2013, things became even riskier for oil exploration companies operating in the Guyanese offshore as Venezuela's thirst for our hydrocarbon grew. In October the Venezuelan navy seized, in Guyana's territorial water, the Teknik Perdana, an oil exploration ship contracted by the US company Anadarko.

The courage and determination of Esso Exploration and Production Guyana Limited (EEPGL), the local affiliate of Exxon Mobil, must be commended in going forward with its planned exploration campaign. Faced not only with the existing risks but also the declining global oil price, the company pressed on leading to the May 2015 'world-class discovery' at Liza 1 in the Stabroek Block.

The exploration company's subsequent discoveries did not come at a small price tag. The 12 discoveries by ExxonMobil amount to in excess of six billion barrels of oil and yet to be officially confirmed stupendous amount of gas to power the country, make Guyana a regional industrial hub and even an exporter.

Playing catch-up

Are we ready for oil prime time? Or more specifically, are we ready for an economy where the oil and gas sector can be the tallest pillar? And to answer the obvious question – what did we do to prepare for commercial oil production in Guyana?

With limited resources there was only so much realistically that could have been done ahead of a commercial discovery curve. However, not lacking was the political will and national enthusiasm to get our nation in shape for this new, exciting bonanza sector.

And so with all that we have now confirmed, and with all the loud buzz and much hype about March 2020 (or before as can be the case), when the first barrel of oil is pumped up and piped into a tanker for refining, we are racing against time. So putting our house in full order cannot be deferred nor delayed.

Can Guyana turn its economy round?

For centuries the productive pillars of the Guyana economy have been agriculture, fishing, mining and forestry. Then, in recent decades, we saw efforts at diversification with bold steps taken to develop the services sector with tourism and information and communication technology as the main areas of focus.

Now with oil production set to commence in a matter of months, we ought to be culturally adaptive as a people for this additional new exciting economic endeavour and its expected interface with the traditional sectors.

But let us think deeply about this: the doubling of gross domestic product by one new sector (oil) can dwarf the impact of the other economic streams. Or even an astronomical growth in state revenue by this single new sector can create shock-waves for the other sectors both in terms of government's priority or even ordinary Guyanese interest in continued participation and investment by the private sector.

Oil revenue, according to an International Monetary Fund forecast, will initially be $350m per annum (and this is conservative as the spin off benefits are not accounted for). Examples abound of how societies in all continents were improved, deformed and/or just simply transformed since commercial oil production began in 1840s in Pennsylvania, USA and Baku, Azerbaijan in 1871.

Gladly, we can all have faith the Guyanese people's ability to rise to the occasion. Our history has proven that we are a versatile and resilient people. Our cultural fabric, I am sure, will be able to adjust. Being aware and prepare, we must! Change should not be feared but rather be embraced with full knowledge of its impact.

It's Guyana's oil, not another's feast...

With Guyana on the verge of being the next Caricom (Caribbean Economic Community) oil and gas giant, we see Trinidad & Tobago (T&T) in overdrive mode to lecture and influence/infiltrate our course of development of this new sector, aided and abetted by some local players. Guyana, like a new beauty, is suddenly dazzling the eyes of our T&T counterparts and others whom are less bold.

There is, however, a feeling of entitlement by some in T&T vis-a-vis Guyana's oil and gas. A recent publication by Anthony Bryan of the University of the West Indies reflected an emerging mindset that our O&G sector should be seen as a feast for Trinidad & Tobago (Bryan, 2017). The article strikes a condescending tone, enumerates the perceived ills and problems of our society and, as we say, gave us 'a good bad mouthing' packaged as an analysis.

Our policy makers and private sector must be on guard. T&T is being very aggressive as it aims to get a chunk of the Guyanese O&G cake, potentially at the disadvantage of our own interests.

So what should we do?

We must continue to encourage T&T, other Caricom states and countries with experience in O&G to invest and provide technical support, where necessary. This is not an excuse to dominate.

There must be a cap on employment of non-Guyanese when these skills are available coupled with an aggressive multi-stakeholder programme on relevant skills development. Encouraging has been the ongoing collaboration between the University of Guyana (UG) and the Ministry of Natural Resources/Department of Energy to train students at UG.

The O&G companies must give preferential treatment or reserve services for qualified local suppliers, which are building experience and capacity for this new sector. T&T has 109 years of experience in oil and gas so its companies will, at this juncture, beat any local company on the requirements for experience and capacity.

A special incubation programme should be implemented for nascent local companies to build experience, expertise and capacity to adequately serve the sector.

Multinationals working in the O&G sector should be discouraged from working through their T&T affiliates and, instead, directly pursue joint ventures and collaboration with reputable Guyanese companies.

A special fund (revolving loans at concessionary rates) needs to be created to assist small and emerging businesses to support and work in the O&G sector.

We see, in other places, where the exclusion of nationals and local businesses in the O&G sector led to severe social and political repercussions.

Finalisation of a local content framework to ensure meaningful participation of Guyanese and Guyanese businesses in the oil and gas sectors. Already, a UK expert has been hired to assist in the effort.

Expedite the building of robust regulatory framework with modern and relevant legislation revision and additions, particularly the creation of the Petroleum Commission.

Stricter enforcement of all relevant regulations and laws concerning the oil and gas sector and holding oil companies accountable, including the promulgation of a depletion policy.

Let's not be naïve. Others are looking at our O&G sector for their next meal. We must demand our fair and just share. But, at the same time, we must be cognisant of the risks and work for the long-term viability of an O&G sector thus enabling us for prime time as a serious player. It is Guyana's oil, not someone else's feast!

Conclusion

Opportunities and threats abound as this new sector emerges to augment other traditional and existing social and economic activities to reshape the economic landscape of Guyana. Let's be cognisant that the road ahead can be slippery. But a paradise is closer if we are able to summon the national courage and will to address our historic political ailments through constitutional reform, a refocus on shared prosperity and national unity, and greater respect from those afar who seek to dictate by either wilful economic influence or sheer disparagement of developing countries such as ours.

Oil will be ours to determine whether it will be a curse or cure. And I'm confident it will be one of the many cures to our decades-old social and economic setbacks. The work of attaining the elusive goal of national prosperity has now started with the beckoning of oil and gas!

Reference

Bryan, Anthony 2017, https://theconversation.com/guyana-one-of-south-americas-poorest-countries-struck-oil-will-it-go-boom-or-bust-86108

About the contributor

Robert M. Persaud (www.robertmpersaud.com) is the former Cabinet Minister of Natural Resources and the Environment in Guyana. He was in office until May 2015. He is now a consultant and a local content advocate.

Chapter 8

The need for parliamentary oversight

**Missteps in early petro law making must not be repeated if
Guyana is to reap all the potential benefits of its new
oil resource, writes Sanjeev Datadin**

Guyana is a small English-speaking country in South America. It has for its
entire existence since independence from Great Britain on the 26 May 1966
been listed amongst the poorest countries in the northern hemisphere.
However, in May 2015 Exxon Mobil struck oil off Guyana's coast in its
territorial waters. The discovery promises to change the status of Guyana
as a poor country and the livelihood of its citizens.

This chapter outlines the legal and regulatory framework in existence in
Guyana as it embarks upon its exploitation of its petroleum reserves.

Background

Guyana was formerly British Guiana, a British colony, which principally
relied on sugar, rice, bauxite and gold as the pillars of its economy. Guyana
is classified as a common law jurisdiction. Guyana is a Commonwealth
country and its legal system is founded upon the English legal system that
it inherited from its colonial past.

Its Westminster-export model constitution and legal system is still closely
associated with the English system. Guyana has an executive president and
a single-chamber parliament unlike most of its sister nations in the
Commonwealth.

Guyana has had petroleum exploration on its shores since the 1930s with
exploration ventures focused mainly in two areas:

- onshore, in the Takutu Basin in the central and southern region of
  Guyana; and
- offshore, off the northern coast of Guyana in the Atlantic Ocean.

It was widely reported that Hunt Oil discovered some petroleum in the Takutu Basin in the 1980s. The current spate of exploration was commenced by CGX, a company traded on the Canadian Stock Market, about a decade ago. This spate of explorations culminated in Exxon's discovery in May 2015.

Legal and regulatory framework

In 2015 the only legislation specifically related to petroleum exploration was the Petroleum (Production) Act and the Petroleum (Exploration and Production) Act 1986. The Petroleum (Production) Act came into being in 1939 and vests all petroleum resources in the state and makes all exploration and production exclusively the right of the state.

The Petroleum (Exploration and Production) Act 1986 added a legislative framework for the state to grant licences and permits related to the exploration and production of petroleum in Guyana. It provided, in very basic terms, a framework for the state to exploit its petroleum reserves by licensing its rights to private and/or foreign entities and receive royalties and other fees in return.

The discovery of vast and lucrative petroleum reserves has meant exploration and its associated march to full production is progressing at breakneck speed – and Guyana is struggling to get its legislative and regulatory framework in place quickly enough to assure it takes maximum social and financial advantage of the exploitation of its petroleum resources. Despite the 1986 Act being widely acknowledged as being inadequate, almost four years since Exxon's discovery there is still no legislation approved by Parliament to provide a more comprehensive framework for exploration and production to take place.

Licensing

All licensing matters in relation to the petroleum industry is governed by the Petroleum (Exploration and Production) Act 1986.

The Act provides for a simple menu of matters to guide petroleum exploration and production. It commences with the application for a prospecting licence (section 20). Once the prospecting licence is granted (in accordance with section 21) and prospecting commences the licensee is obliged to notify the state about any discovery of oil (section 30) and a specific notification if oil is discovered in commercial quantities (section 31). Once commercial quantities are discovered then the holder of the prospecting licence must apply for a production licence (section 34). Finally, a production licence is granted (in accordance with section 35).

The initial production licence is for a maximum period of 20 years, with renewal being for a period not exceeding 10 years. The production licence addresses diverse matters such as the area where the holder can operate, the obligation to do a fixed set of work, right sell or otherwise dispose of petroleum recovered and execute other production and prospecting works promised at the time of the grant of the licence.

Establishing local companies

Licenses can only be granted to a company whether local or foreign. Guyana's company law regime is closely aligned to the Canadian companies legislation, i.e. the Canadian Business Corporations Act.

Incorporation of a private company is inexpensive and takes less than a week. To incorporate a company the principal requirements are as follows:

- The purpose(s) of the business
- The name of the incorporators (at least one) is required
- The name of the director(s) (minimum one) and secretary of the company
- The registered office of the business
- The proposed by-laws of the business.

The registration of foreign companies is again inexpensive and equally fast. This creates a local branch of a foreign company and may be convenient for tax and administrative purposes.

Local content

Guyana's new buzzwords since the discovery of oil in 2015 have been 'local content' – the active desire of the citizens and local businessmen to be a part of the oil industry and get a share of the wealth it promises.

There is no legislation in place for local content and there appears to be no plans for legislation to be enacted in this regard. However, the second draft of the Local Content and Value Addition Policy Framework (the Local Content Framework) has been in circulation since May 2018.

The sloth in developing and implementing a comprehensive policy is not to the benefit of Guyana. Exploration and the advancement to production in the Atlantic blocks off the Guyana coast are progressing quickly and the absence of a policy delays the locals' ability to benefit in the manner envisaged and indeed promised by the Government. There is need also for a supervising agency/body to oversee the implementation of a local content policy and to investigate and ascertain that the foreign companies are observing the policy.

The usual local content 'advantages' are at risk because of the absence of a regulatory framework and a supervising agency. In the property rental market, for example, the absence of a restriction on foreign companies owning property would mean that the foreign companies would purchase property and build structures to suit their needs as opposed to renting from local property owners. This would invariably lead to inflated prices for in-demand locations as locals would struggle to compete with the deep pockets of the large foreign companies.

The Local Content Framework is the best indication of the policies and standards the state will insist upon as regards local content. At present, in accordance with the Local Content Framework, 'locals' are persons who are Guyanese citizens or legal residents; for companies it would apply to companies that are more than 50 per cent beneficially owned by a Guyanese national. The focus is on the training of persons with the necessary skills for the petroleum industry. The Local Content Framework is still a work in progress and will hopefully be settled soon.

Supervising authority

The framework for the supervision and decision making in relation to the petroleum exploration and production in Guyana is very hodge-podge at the moment. The Government has not achieved the clear and distinct channels of decision-making preferred for such a crucial industry to Guyana's future.

The Ministry of Natural Resources initially was the body with the responsibility to oversee the petroleum industry in Guyana and its minister was the key player in negotiations with the foreign oil companies, including the much criticised Exxon Production Sharing Agreement (Exxon PSA).

There has been a Bill in Parliament since 2017 to establish a Petroleum Commission but it has not yet passed. The Petroleum Commission to be established under the Bill was in fact set up (despite the law not being passed) but now seems to no longer be on the Government's agenda.

The new path appears to be the Energy Department that has absorbed some of the staff of the Petroleum Commission. The department, when announced, coincided with a move of the petroleum industry away from the Ministry of Natural Resources to the Ministry of the Presidency. The department, peculiarly, is expressed to be not under the portfolio of the Minister in the Ministry of the Presidency, leaving its supervision to the President directly. The absence of clear lines of direction and control is most unfortunate and places Guyana at a disadvantage.

Wealth fund

The national consensus seems to have been for the establishment of a sovereign wealth fund to manage the petroleum revenue so as to maximise its benefits and provide for future generations.

The Guyana Natural Resources Bill 2018 was passed in Parliament on 3 January 2019. It establishes the fund and provides for its supervision and management. However, the Act is not free from controversy.

On 21 December 2018 a no-confidence motion (NCM) tabled by the Opposition was passed. The Government fell on that day. The Constitution of Guyana (Articles 106 and 107) mandated that the Cabinet of Guyana must resign and general elections be held within three months.

The passage of legislation in such circumstances was unorthodox to say the least; but it was passed and remains so, at least for now. It was unfortunate that such important legislation was passed in a parliamentary sitting at which the Opposition was absent.

The future

The need for a complete legislative framework for the petroleum industry in Guyana is beyond doubt. There should be clear and fixed guidelines to bind everyone equally. Only an established legal and regulatory framework can achieve this in a fair way. The alternative can be disastrous.

The fear of a lack of transparency and outright corruption would not be properly addressed without such a framework. This framework should address everything from the content requirements of future production-sharing agreements to what duty-free concessions can be granted.

The negotiation of contracts by established civil servants with some form of parliamentary oversight must be encouraged. Only then will the debacle of the Exxon PSA be avoided in the future. This PSA with the Guyana

Government provided for tax-free concessions for Exxon and all its suppliers, audit requirements with short timelines, and without the ability of the Government to effectively obtain source documents and, of course, the much criticised mere $18m signing bonus.

The challenges are real and are likely to have grave consequences unless resolved. The Exxon PSA, for example, provides for the financial audits to be conducted within a fixed-time frame otherwise it is taken to have been accepted by the state.

In simple terms, Exxon submits its bills to the Government of the amount it has expended on exploration and production that it is entitled to deduct from the total production figures, Guyana has the right to audit these figures but must do so in a fixed period of time. The observance of these timelines is crucial to Guyana getting its maximum benefit.

Additionally, mechanisms to monitor the flow of oil should be implemented by Guyana independently of Exxon. This would mean installing flow meters on every oil rig engaged in production.

This is imperative so that the Government can, in real time, ascertain exactly how many barrels of petroleum has been produced at any given time making its calculation of royalties and fees much more accurate and pain free. Additionally, with much of the expenses of Exxon being recoverable as a charge against production costs (which is essentially paid by Guyana) care must be had to supervise the services engaged by Exxon on matters such as airline travel, training personnel and educating the children of its employees.

The persistent media reports that airfare cost on a foreign airline is a multiple of all the others, similarly with education costs at a local school. This must be addressed and kept to a reasonable figure; it is only with a regulatory framework and supervising agency in place that these excesses would be reined in or altogether eliminated.

The focus should not be, as it is at the present, to somehow re-do the Exxon PSA, but to make sure the missteps of that contract are not repeated in the future. The only effective was to do that would be to remove the one-on-one style negotiations that have been taking place between the Government and oil companies and make the terms and conditions of all agreements be provided for in legislation and/or regulation.

About the contributor

Sanjeev Datadin is an Attorney-at-Law practising across the Caribbean for 22 years. He is the Founding Partner of Whitworth Chambers. He has appeared in the courts of Guyana, Trinidad and Tobago and the Eastern Caribbean and has extensive appellate experience in the Caribbean Court of Justice and the Judicial Committee of the Privy Council. He has also practised at the Chambre Maritime Arbitrale in Paris and the Court of Arbitration for Sport in Lausanne, Switzerland.

Chapter 9

'The Petroleum Commission – an investment in Guyana's Future'

Guyana stands on the cusp of amazing transformational change. Having worked in the international oil industry for more than 38 years, Sally Gibson is now bearing witness to the emergence of Guyana's oil and gas industry in the country of her birth

A fit-for-purpose legislative and regulatory framework is a necessary requirement for the development of Guyana's petroleum resources. This is a recognised part of the 'Energy Value Chain' which provides a framework for the delivery of the sustainable development of oil and gas resources.

The industry regulator is a fundamental part of the regulatory framework and a Bill was laid before the National Assembly in May 2017 to establish the Petroleum Commission. The Bill's progress has been slow and it is understood that the legislation is currently delayed until the petroleum legislation is updated.

Certain parts of the Bill as originally laid emerged as controversial following the public consultation process. In particular, the establishment of the board of directors, powers of the minister and remuneration of staff, which were considered to detract from the independence of the Commission as a regulatory body. There have since been moves to address these concerns.

The aim is not to turn these stones over since they have been subject to much public comment, but to consider the key drivers for the successful and efficient delivery of a regulator's functions.

Petroleum regulator

The industry regulator occupies a key strategic position in energy-sector development. It holds responsibility for petroleum regulation and the monitoring and enforcement of petroleum activities. It has a critical role in promoting resource management to enable petroleum resources to be developed sustainably in the public interest. It also provides stakeholder re-assurance and acts as an enabler to investment by providing regulatory certainty and in ensuring transparency, accountability and competitiveness when performing its duties.

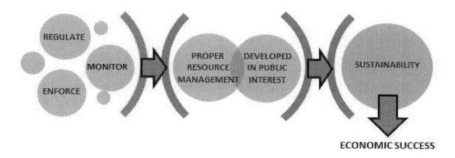

Guyana's Petroleum Commission

The Petroleum Commission's over-arching function as set out in the original draft Bill is:

> 'To monitor and regulate the efficient, safe, effective and environmentally responsible exploration, development and production of petroleum'.

This is comprehensive as a motherhood statement, but the Commission's more specific duties include:

1. enforcing the terms of licences, PSCs, joint venture agreements and ensuring compliance with policy, laws and regulations;
2. making recommendations on applications for petroleum prospecting and production licences and managing bid rounds;
3. regulating and monitoring petroleum activities and ensuring that competition and fair practice is maintained;
4. reviewing and advising the Government on all petroleum activities, making recommendations on developments plans and production forecasts and ensuring the optimal utilisation of existing/planned facilities;

5. promoting efficiency, conservation and safety in petroleum activities and environmental operations and ensuring well-planned, well-executed and cost-efficient operations;
6. assessing cost oil and gas and collecting royalties, levies and other charges payable under the Petroleum Acts;
7. promoting local content and local participation in petroleum activities.

The Commission is required to carry out its functions in line with the energy policies of the Government. The function of a petroleum regulator is to regulate and monitor the development of a nation's resources and compliance with government policy is reflected in industry practice.

Great expectations?

Simple compliance with statutory duties does not necessarily make for a successful regulator. Stating the obvious, a good regulator has to be credible and earn public trust and confidence. The golden thread which should run through the organisation and be embedded in its culture is (a) good governance; and (b) the efficient stewardship of resources in an economically sustainable way.

Good governance

Transparency and accountability are key to good governance. These can easily fall by the wayside as sound bites so leadership and the participation of stakeholders are required to drive them as part of the democratic process. The aim should be for a 'win-win' outcome since organisations, which are transparent and accountable, tend to demonstrate a greater compliance with the rule of law and command a higher level of public trust and confidence.

The challenge for newly emerging oil countries is to deliver good governance. The draft Bill gives the Commission the tool box to enable delivery but it has to be shown that the theory can be turned into practice.

Looking at the requirements for transparency, the draft Bill requires the Commission to be open and objective and ensure transparency in its activities and in the petroleum sector. The promotion of competitiveness, the reporting of data, the maintenance of proper books and records and compliance with international financial standards are also key requirements.

In terms of accountability, an annual report detailing petroleum activities is required to be published. Details of local content and local participation, petroleum production, royalty and fees paid and HSE matters are also to be included. The requirements to promote competition, keep books and records and comply with financial standards also goes to the heart of accountability.

History will judge whether good governance has been effectively implemented. That said, effective leadership and political will needs to drive the agenda from inception otherwise good governance will fall at the first hurdle.

Efficient stewardship

Competition and collaboration have been shown to be fundamental to the efficient stewardship of petroleum resources.

Fostering **competition** is important since it helps to promote the efficient allocation of resources which in turn leads to **economic growth**. Facilitating **competition** is one instrument for overcoming **market power and levelling** the imbalances that may exist and licensing rounds are an example of the effective use of competition in the industry.

Once again, the draft Bill provides the tool box since the Commission is required to promote competitiveness in carrying out its functions and duties including facilitating competition, access and the use of petroleum facilities by third parties.

Collaboration and co-operation between all stakeholders have shown demonstrable results in achieving the enhanced delivery of resources, efficiencies in petroleum activities and the supply chain together with a more efficient use of infrastructure and facilities.

By way of example, in the establishing the UK Oil and Gas Authority (OGA), collaboration was recognised as key to delivering the 'Principal Objective' of maximising the economic recovery of petroleum, so much so, that the requirement to collaborate was included in the Petroleum Act 1998 as a statutory obligation.

This requirement is treated very seriously and the OGA has recently published a guide which includes collaborative behavioural assessment tools so that organisations can demonstrate how they are meeting their collaboration requirements.

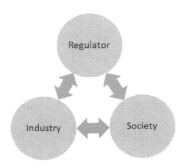

Collaboration requires the regulator, industry and society to work together in a solid partnership. It is recognised that different competing interests can potentially hinder the process. The UK OGA has shown that it can achieve measurable and successful outcomes through focus on the requirement for industry and government to maximise the economic recovery of petroleum in the public interest.

Hope for the future?

Collaboration requires the regulator, industry and society to work together in a solid partnership. It is recognised that different competing interests can potentially hinder the process. The UK OGA has shown that it can achieve measurable and successful outcomes through focus on the requirement for industry and government to maximise the economic recovery of petroleum in the public interest.

As an emerging producer, Guyana possesses a vast amount of political and social energy. The hope is that it will be able to harness this whilst maintaining the balance between openness and effectiveness. First oil is expected as early as the end of 2019 and the Petroleum Commission remains a critical piece of the jigsaw waiting to be put in place.

About the contributor

Sally Gibson a qualified barrister, is a highly regarded international energy lawyer with more than 38 years' experience of the oil and gas sector. During her early career Sally worked for a number of international oil companies before forming her own independent energy consultancy, Petro-Legal Limited, which she has managed successfully for the last 24 years. She has worked with private and state-owned companies and negotiated contracts with host governments as well as international oil companies.

Chapter 10

Will oil ruin or make Guyana? The lessons from Trinidad

Guyana is not unique in the Caribbean region for enjoying big oil finds. Neighbour Venezuela has the world's largest reserves while Trinidad and Tobago has had oil for more than a century. What can Guyana learn from Trinidad and Tobago, asks John Mair.

There has been a massive find of oil in offshore Guyana, possibly the biggest in South America for decades. Already, Exxon Mobil has announced five billion barrels from 12 discoveries, with the total expected to climb to a potential 10bn barrels once others declare their finds in other fields.

Guyana will be gushing with oil from its sea beds from 2020. Then it is expected that output will start at 120,000 barrels a day, rising to 750,000 by 2025. The revenue for the country could be $5-10bn (all figures in US dollars) per year by the middle of the next decade.

Guyana could be the new Nigeria...or the new Norway.

Black gold – or not?

How much of that oil money will land in the country? Lower estimates vary as low as $100m per year (half the annual amount from remittances sent home by overseas Guyanese) and the creation of just 1000-2000 jobs in a country of 750,000 with heavy unemployment, little manufacturing industry and a sugar industry in its death throes.

High estimates say that oil will make Guyana rich. At the current market price of around $60 per barrel the country can expect to net $1m a day in oil earnings Break-even point for Guyanese oil is low, success rates in finding it high.

61

What can Guyana learn from other Caribbean countries where oil has come and nearly gone, especially Trinidad & Tobago?

Let us attempt to draw lessons for Guyana in terms of economics, social structure and politics gained through the 'Trini' experience. Was it all good, all bad? Who gained and who lost? How do you avoid their mistakes?

Thanks to oil, Guyana could be among the richest countries in the world in a decade or two. Deep-water surveys estimate of Guyana's oil at 10bn barrels pales in comparison to neighbouring Venezuela but surpasses the reserves of Trinidad & Tobago, long the Caribbean Community's (Caricom) biggest oil producer.

T&T: more than 100 years in oil and gas

Trinidad is a mature oil and natural gas producer. The first oil wells were drilled in 1856 and commercial production began in December 1907. By 1996, revenue from natural gas exceeded that from oil production and Trinidad embarked on a massive scale of industrialisation.

Today the country is home to more than 100 petrochemical industries. The Point Lisas estate, with eight methanol plants (including the largest in the world), has become the globe's major exporter of ammonium, and is the fifth largest exporter of LNG (liquid natural gas) in the world.

T&T became the most dynamic and wealthiest economy in the Caribbean because of oil riches. In T&T the economy is highly dependent on the energy sector which accounts for 45.3 per cent of its GDP, provides 57.5 per cent of government revenue, and is responsible for 83 per cent of merchandise exports

But that was the zenith of its oil boom. That summit has been reached and past. Since reality has set in and the oil and gas sector has contracted.

In August 2018 the state oil refinery announced it would be closing with the loss of 1700 jobs. Petrotrin has lost a total of about T&T$8bn in the last five years, is T&T$12bn in debt; and owes the Government of Trinidad & Tobago more than T&T$3bn in taxes and royalties. It had been refining oil below cost price for years.

Lessons for Guyana

What can Guyana learn from the experience of her fellow Caricom state. I talked to some of those most closely involved in the management of the industry and study of it. (See my acknowledgements). Here is a distillation of their wisdom.

1. Establish an independently managed sovereign wealth fund: Norway is the shining example of one that works. There are many not-so-good examples. Guyana has started the process but it appears stalled.

2. Avoid the 'resource curse': From Iran to Nigeria, worldwide experience confirms that social conflict and economic instability result when income from drilling, mining and the like is unequally distributed. Guyana must move quickly to avoid this 'curse'.

3. Avoid boom and bust: Complete reliance on the energy sector is a recipe for boom and bust cycles with the accompanying social and political disruptions. In Trinidad the end of the 20th century witnessed a new boom and bust period beginning to emerge. The global financial crisis of 2008 triggered a collapse of oil and gas prices and since then T&T has had to face another boom-and-bust cycle.

Guyana as a new deep water oil province would do well to use the largesse from oil to enter directly and early to renewable energy (solar, hydro etc). Oil is finite, renewable is not.

4. Establish public (state) companies to manage the industry: These companies must be insulated from political influence. The Norway Statoil model of appointing board members is instructive. Make shares in these companies available to the public via IPOs and APOs.

5. Create the right climate for investment for private companies: From the perspective of the international oil companies (IOCs) T&T became a model for energy investment.

6. Transparency is all: Make data available to the public without breaching confidentiality provisions of contracts. Guyana has not had a good start with the $18m 'signing on' fee from Exxon which was hidden from view for 17 months.

7. Ensure the oil wealth trickles down to the people: In T&T, San Fernando and Central Trinidad (Chaguanas) have done very well economically. For better or for worse their urban lifestyles rival the Port of Spain metropolitan area including the East-West corridor.

8. Look to the future after oil: Go downstream of oil and natural gas to maximise the value that accrues to Guyana from its depleting resource.

Build your non-oil industries using the proceeds from both oil and natural gas.

9. Look after your pristine backyard: Maritime crude drilling goes hand in hand with leaky pipelines, ruptured barges and rig malfunctions. Protect against this by law before it is too late.

10. **Focus on human development for the sector:** Not just university educated people but technicians. Guyana has a literate and educated population in and out of the country. Use them.

Conclusion

Guyana is a neophyte oil power. The gush of discoveries has been relentless and swift. The country has to play catch up on all fronts with some speed. Trinidad & Tobago provides some directions –positive and negative – for the way forward.

Acknowledgments

With thanks for their input to Kevin Ramnarine, former T&T Energy Minister; Professor Anthony Bryan of UWI; Ambassador Riyad Insanally, formerly OAS Ambassador in T&T now in Washington for the Government of Guyana; and Christopher Ram, chartered accountant/lawyer and a recognised sage on oil in Guyana.

About the contributor

John Mair is Guyanese by birth, British by nationality. He visits his 'motherland' frequently. He is a former BBC producer who has taught university and edited (to date) 30 books on matters journalistic. *Anti-Social Media?* was published in Autumn 2018. Since then he has masterminded a series on Brexit with *Do They Mean Us?* and *The Case for Brexit* already published.

Chapter 11

Lessons from Venezuela

Venezuela's slide from top of the heap to a virtual bit player in the oil market is a slow-motion car crash. Production sank progressively from 2.6m barrels per day (b/d) a decade ago, when it was third in Opec behind only Saudi Arabia and Iran, to 2m b/d by Q3 2017. Decline since has been precipitous – today it's just 1.1m b/d, says Simon Flowers, in an article originally published in *Forbes*

The market has shrugged off the loss, even with the absence of sanctioned Iranian oil. Venezuela's heavy barrels have been largely displaced by supplies from Canada, Mexico and elsewhere.

As the US sanctions announced January 28 bite, worse lies ahead. Two factors will drive production down to 0.7m b/d over the next six months in our latest forecasts: lack of access to the diluent needed to help the heavy crude flow; and limited availability of finance for workovers and basic maintenance on wells, The intensifying economic squeeze and external political pressure will likely lead to a new government and stabilisation in 2020. Then, perhaps, recovery can begin.

The collapse of the economy has been one of the most severe (barring wars) since the fall of the Soviet Union. Six years ago, GDP per person was $14,500, placing Venezuela just behind Chile as the wealthiest economy in South America and in the top 50 globally. In the past five years, the size of the economy has roughly halved. Besides severe recession, the country is grappling with hyperinflation and a population exodus. The UN estimates that some 3m of the country's 31m people have fled since 2015.

A central factor in the shrivelling of the economy has been over-dependence on oil. Non-oil industries have all but vanished, their share of exports falling from around 25 per cent in the late 1990s to less than 3 per cent in recent years. The Government borrowed heavily against rising oil revenues in the previous decade, fuelling social spending. When oil prices fell in 2014, Venezuela had minimal savings and no other buffer. The result has been a shortage of dollars to pay for imports of even basic goods, never mind repaying its international creditors or maintaining oil production.

It's a window to a dystopian future for Guyana. Venezuela's neighbour to the east, Guyana is developing its first offshore oil and gas finds made in the past four years. There's a growing number of them; the 11th and 12th announced last week takes resource to over 5bn barrels of oil equivalent, most of it oil and low cost. Production could exceed 1m b/d next decade, putting Guyana in non-Opec's top ten – from nowhere. Operator ExxonMobil's plan for the Liza complex will transform the economy.

Discipline is required

Guyana's GDP was $3.7bn (all figures in US dollars) in 2017, but will grow by multiples. Our analysis of the upstream project assumes total investment of over $30bn; plateauing at $5bn annually in the early 2020s as the known discoveries are developed; all perhaps matched by investment down the value chain onshore. Tax revenues kick in from the mid-2020s and build up quickly to more than $10bn a year.

For such a small economy, the scale of development is staggering. Assuming oil production of 1m b/d by 2030, Guyana's output per person will be higher than any other major oil producer. A four-fold increase in the size of its economy over a decade is possible, catapulting Guyana into the high-income bracket. Azerbaijan and Equatorial Guinea are other countries in recent history that have experienced similar explosive growth, but from a lower base.

What can Guyana do to make the most of its oil and avoid the pitfalls? Kuwait and the UAE have consistently invested a portion of revenues in sovereign wealth funds. Each had built up a buffer three to four times the size of their economies to draw on when the oil price collapsed in 2014. Such a strategy helps smooth out the boom and bust, but requires a high degree of discipline. It will be tempting to spend, spend, spend.

Another clear lesson from Venezuela is not to become too dependent on a single source of revenue. Building infrastructure and raising education standards will facilitate development of other sectors. Local content and employment requirements for the oil industry can support this process.

It will be a delicate balancing act. The role of government is also central to success in setting clear energy policy, establishing firm and independent regulation, and a stable fiscal policy. These set a framework for close collaboration with international operators. The fate of Venezuela is all the incentive needed to get this right.

Source: *Forbes*

About the contributor

Simon Flowers is Chief Analyst and Chairman of Wood Mackenzie. He has more than 20 years of experience in the oil, gas, utilities and mining sectors, working with the boards of many energy companies on strategic issues. His views on major industry issues are regularly sought by the media in Europe, the US and Asia. Simon graduated in geology from the University of Edinburgh, and worked for two years as a geologist in the oil industry working in the Netherlands and offshore Egypt. He is based in Edinburgh.

Chapter 12

Lessons from Aberdeen

Mark Lammey says that Guyana can learn much from the experiences of the oil capital of the UK

Black Gold has been the cornerstone of Aberdeen's economy for decades, providing an anchor for high skilled, high value jobs. That's the view of the authors of Aberdeen City Council's inaugural economic policy panel report, published in November 2018. It would be difficult to find anyone who would challenge that assessment.

The industry has undeniably reshaped the Granite City's landscape in the years that followed the first gas discovery in the mid-1960s. Pockets and clusters of offices and manufacturing facilities occupied by oil producers and engineering firms are dotted around the city, which has earned the title of Europe's Energy Capital. And nearby Westhill is known as Surf City for its hosting of the continent's largest cluster of subsea businesses.

An extensive study by consultancy Xodus Group said 'respect, experience, depth, quality, confidence, assurance and efficiency' were all used regularly to describe the Scottish subsea engineering industry. The report went further in saying the 'breadth of experience and the depth of the talent pool' in the subsea sector was a 'key factor to the success of the region'.

Guyana can look to harness this skill and expertise to assist with the development of its emerging offshore oil and gas industry.

The cornerstone of an economy

Oil and gas can form the bedrock of a resilient economy, which supports a range of other sectors, whether that's hospitality, food and drink or transport, for example.

More than 27,000 people were directly employed in the oil and gas sector in the north-east of Scotland in 2017, representing 75.3 per cent of all direct oil and gas employment in Great Britain, the council's report said. The researchers estimated that oil and gas 'supports' as many as 86,000 jobs in the region. Without doubt, the oil industry is also the main driver of the north-east's high productivity, which eclipses levels seen in the rest of the country.

Aberdeen's productivity was measured at £36.30 gross value added (GVA) per hour in 2016, compared to £32.58 for the UK. Indeed, in the north-east, productivity has consistently been above the UK average and among the highest of all Scottish regions.

It's clear that Big Oil's decision to put down roots in Aberdeen has had a marked social impact on a city which was once better known for fishing. The city has a reputation for being one of the most expensive places to live in the UK, with high property prices, but also higher wages. In 2016, gross disposable household income per head for Aberdeen was £22,508, compared to £18,231 for Scotland.

Pioneering spirit lives on

A pioneering spirit was cultivated during the early years of North Sea exploration in one of the world's harshest basins. And there is plenty of evidence to suggest that Aberdeen's innovative soul is alive and well today.

Aberdeen is the top city in Scotland and in the top 10 UK city regions for business start-ups, according to Aberdeen and Grampian Chamber of Commerce (AGCC). Research by Barclays and the Business Growth Fund supports the chamber's view, claiming Aberdeen was the most entrepreneurial city in Scotland in 2014, after the number of new enterprises rose higher compared to Glasgow and Edinburgh.

In 2016, there were 60.1 patent applications per 100,000 people in Aberdeen, more than three times higher than the UK average, the council said in its report. Research and development spend per person in Aberdeen was £717 in 2016, head and shoulders above the Scottish national average of £198.

Aberdeen is well positioned to build on its reputation for innovation, with £180m being invested in the new Oil and Gas Technology Centre over 10 years. What's more, Aberdeen has consistently attracted high levels of inward investment and was in ninth place in the league of UK cities of foreign direct investment projects, with 14 projects in 2017.

It could perhaps be concluded that if a city or region can earn a reputation for innovation, that track record can crystallise and persist and for a prolonged period.

The oil industry could do the same for Guyana.

Biggest show in town

Aberdeen hosts some of the top oil and gas industry conferences and exhibitions, most notably, Offshore Europe, every two years, and the annual Subsea Expo. Offshore Europe is the Eastern Hemisphere's largest oil production and exploration event and has been held in Aberdeen since 1973.

The four-day show contributed a substantial £53.9m to the regional economy in 2013 and was attended by a record 63,000 people. This year it will be staged at the new £333m TECA conference centre near Aberdeen International Airport.

A total of 6,500 people from around the word, including the US, Middle East, South America, Africa and Asia attended the most recent Subsea Expo, which celebrates the UK's £7.5bn subsea sector.

Industry organisations Oil and Gas UK, Subsea UK and the Society of Petroleum Engineers all host awards ceremonies attended and participated in by thousands of energy sector professionals. If nothing else, this indicates that the international oil and gas community is ready and willing to travel in huge numbers to promote their businesses and make new connections.

Guyana should capitalise on the enthusiasm for adventure and discovery.

Being a good neighbour

Plenty of the oil and gas companies which have nested in Aberdeen give something back to the community. Baker Hughes, a GE company has sponsored a popular 10 kilometre race through Aberdeen, which is participated in by thousands of people, for more than three decades. The 10K was born out of the city's annual marathon, but eventually superseded that event when it was discontinued a few years later.

Royal Dutch Shell runs the Girls in Energy programme, a one-year course designed to open young women's eyes to the energy industry's wealth of career opportunities and promote Stem (science, technology, engineering and maths) subjects. As part of the Girls in Energy calendar, Shell hosts a conference in Aberdeen which is attended by 100 schoolgirls every year.

They compete in the Bright Ideas Challenge, a competition to find new ideas and solutions for the energy industry from the next generation.

TechFest – an annual technology festival – has been running for more than a quarter of a century in Aberdeen. Its goal is to engage young people in the Stem subjects and encourage them to go on to follow a career which utilises these skills by demonstrating that they are both fun and relevant in day to day life. Oil majors BP and Shell were joint principal funders of the last year's edition of TechFest.

But it's not just operators and Tier 1 contractors who do their bit. Drilling equipment rental business Saltire Energy has donated more than £8m to both Aberdeen-based and international beneficiaries through its prized Saltire in the Community Programme.

From this, it can be suggested that, when given the right platform, oil and gas companies are willing to concern themselves with their host city or region's future and wider prosperity.

If Guyana can harness this zeal, and ensure that local content (the employment of Guyanese citizens by international oil companies), then society as a whole can benefit.

Get diversification right

The UK oil industry has contributed billions of pounds to the economy over the last five decades, and the North Sea is thought to be capable of producing another 10-20bn barrels. Industry has also come up with Vision 2035, a scenario whereby North Sea industry provides work for another generation of workers.

But Aberdeen was hit extremely hard by the most recent downturn, which started in 2014, but it woke people up to the fact that the north-east needed to develop other industries to share the burden of responsibility with oil and gas.

Arguing the case for a £3bn City Region Deal for Aberdeen in 2015, entrepreneur and philanthropist Sir Ian Wood warned that the city risked becoming a 'bleak museum' to an oil industry which was allowed to decline rapidly and prematurely, and wasn't augmented with anything new.

Sir Ian, who transformed a family-owned fishing business based in Aberdeen into Wood plc, a multinational oil services company, said the alternative was a 'renaissance' for Aberdeen. That vision depended on putting public funding back into the energy sector, improving infrastructure and developing industries such as tourism, food and drink and life sciences.

In its economic report, Aberdeen City Council reasoned that the north-east could not rely on the oil and gas industry to deliver the same scale of benefits into the future, as UK oil production was expected to enter a period of decline in the 2020s. The ambition of its Regional Economic Strategy was to ultimately diversify the economy away from oil and gas in particular and towards growth sectors.

Guyana should learn from this cautionary tale and make sure it thinks of ways in which its oil wealth can be put towards the development of a more rounded, resilient economy.

Many commentators have condemned the UK Government for failing to copy Norway's example and amass a wealth fund from oil revenues, which can be put towards social projects and pension payments.

The difference in population sizes means comparisons between the UK and Norway are unhelpful, but Guyana should be able to create such a fund, reaping the rewards of its natural resources.

About the contributor

Mark Lammey has been the editor of the Energy Voice website and monthly supplement since February 2018. He also worked as a reporter on *The Press & Journal's* business desk for a number of years. He started his career in journalism as the website editor for *The Moscow Times* in the Russian capital.

Chapter 13

A blueprint for sustained success

A disciplined stewardship of the windfall from Guyana's new petroleum finds could lead to great long-term prosperity, says Bobby Gossai, Jr.

Extracting value from offshore petroleum and ensuring operations are conducted to an appropriate standard are more closely linked than is generally acknowledged because they share the same underlying purpose: making the most of a public asset (Chandler 2018).

Therefore, Guyana must manage its offshore operations effectively, since it is an important part of a holistic approach in ensuring that the most value is extracted for the benefits of the operators and the country. Hence, maximising economic rents from the petroleum resources should be the key objective of the Government.

Consequently, with a current reserve of more than five billion barrels of oil and more to be discovered, and with first oil expected in 2020, Guyana must develop a new growth model to transform the potential resource windfall into long-term prosperity. Such a model should have six core elements:

1. Building the institutions and governance of the resources sector;
2. Developing infrastructure;
3. Ensuring robust fiscal policy and competitiveness;
4. Supporting local content;
5. Deciding how to spend a resources windfall wisely;
6. Transforming resource wealth into broader economic development.

Institutions and governance of the resources sector

There is a common view that a government has only two choices in the way it participates in the resources sector: letting private-sector firms operate with minimal involvement from the state beyond taxation and regulation or controlling production through a state-owned company. However, the range of possible government roles is much wider than this, as the following examples illustrate:

- **No state ownership**: In Australia and Canada and elsewhere, the state does not have direct involvement in the industry, but receives taxes or royalties or both.
- **Minority investor**: The state has a minority stake in a company, but does not play an active role in its management or direction.
- **Majority-owned, with limited operatorship**: The state has a majority stake in a company and plays a role in the company's management, but less than 10 per cent of the company's production is operated by the state, or the state operates exclusively in certain segments such as onshore oil.
- **Majority-owned operator**: These companies are fully or majority-owned by the state, and more than 10 per cent of the company's production is operated by the state company.
- **Government monopolist**: Pemex in Mexico and Saudi Aramco in Saudi Arabia are fully owned by the state. Those and other companies in this category account for more than 80 per cent of the country's total production.

The popularity of each type of participation varies according to the resource. Today, more than half of oil and gas producers representing almost three-quarters of world production, are fully or majority state-owned (McKinsey Global Institute 2013). No single model of government participation works best in all countries – countries that have taken the same approach have experienced vastly different levels of success. The best approach depends on the context.

Regardless of the model chosen, there are three guiding principles which are vital for Guyana's successful state participation. First, the Government needs to establish a stable regulatory regime with clear rules and well-defined roles for each player in the sector. Second, it is important to ensure that there is competitive pressure by exposing national operators to private-sector competition, strongly benchmarking performance, or imposing other market disciplines such as scrutiny from private shareholders or bondholders. Finally, the state needs to play a central role in attracting and retaining world-class talent into the sector – even more important if the state chooses to play a more active operational role.

Infrastructure

On average, resource-driven countries such as Guyana do not compare favourably with the rest of the world on their infrastructure, and this often puts investors off (Global Competitiveness Report 2012–2013). This could be particularly challenging given that capital markets are not well developed in many resource-driven countries. However, these economies can help to address the infrastructure imperative by transforming the productivity of infrastructure investment—in other words, they can do more with less. Therefore, Guyana can use three main levers that can help to obtain better infrastructural output: improving project selection and optimising infrastructure portfolios; streamlining delivery; and making the most of existing infrastructure, including sharing it.

The third area is an opportunity for the economy given the large infrastructure requirements of major extractive projects. Given the huge need of the country, Guyana could look closely at ways of sharing infrastructure. By doing so, it can take advantage of private-sector capital and know-how; build stable, long-term partnerships with extractive companies; and achieve broader social benefits from the infrastructure that is put in place. Hence, the Government must think carefully about their approach to resource-related infrastructure to ensure that it provides the maximum benefits to society.

Competitiveness and fiscal policy

Guyana has much to gain from doing all it can to ensure that the petroleum resource sectors are as globally competitive as possible. A robust resource industry creates jobs, contributes to a government's finances through tax and royalty payments, and ensures sustained spending on exploration, increasing the viability of marginal deposits. National competitiveness becomes even more important as major new projects turn out to be more expensive and complex, and as greater volatility in resource prices increases the risk of projects being postponed or cancelled.

However, Guyana should not focus too narrowly on fiscal policy, without considering the broader competitiveness implications for its overall economy. In this context, focus should be on the resource's competitiveness, which encompasses three major elements of competitiveness: production costs, country risk, and the Government 'take' (the share of revenue that accrues to the Government).

This approach takes into account the real economics of projects, including a country's geology and factors such as the availability of infrastructure and regulatory or policy risks. Governments have the ability to affect all three of the elements of competitiveness including, of course, how much of the revenue pie they will take by setting royalties and taxes.

Production costs vary significantly relative to revenue depending on the type of resource and the geology of any particular asset. Costs (as a share of project revenue) are generally higher in mining than in oil and gas and for new sites. This demonstrates that the Government take is closely correlated to production costs. In essence, when production costs are high, the Government take is necessarily lower to ensure that costs are competitive with alternative investments.

This is true for individual resources and across resources. Whilst, a government obviously cannot control factors such as the proximity of resource deposits to the coast, the quality of crude oil, or mineral grades, there are still avenues available to reduce capital and operating costs, especially by focusing on regulation, supply chains, productivity and cooperation with the industry.

Political or regulatory risk (measured as a share of the value of a project) can sometimes amount to a very high per cent of the value of the Government take expressed as a percentage of revenue. This significantly weakens the competitiveness and attractiveness of the country. Even allowing for below optimal levels of government take, this demonstrates the importance of risk to companies.

Hence, there are large opportunities for Guyana to reduce risk by developing its ability to understand and negotiate contracts (ensuring that the contracts are fair and seen to be fair), adopting a set of formal legal mechanisms to help reassure investors, and generally improving interaction with investors and companies.

Guyana will achieve far more by focusing on production costs and reducing risks in collaboration with resource companies than by narrowly focusing on trying to increase the government take. Successfully reducing production costs and risks produces a larger revenue pie that can then be shared by the Government and the resource companies.

Local content development

Beyond generating taxes and royalties, the extractive industry can make substantial contributions to a country's economic development by supporting local employment and supply chains. Between 40 and 80 per cent of the revenue created in oil and gas is spent on the procurement of goods and services, often exceeding tax and royalty payments in some cases. Increasing the proportion of goods and services that are procured locally ('local content') will be a key goal for policy makers in the resource-driven economy of Guyana.

If the local-content regulations are designed poorly, they can substantially reduce the competitiveness of the resources sector, endangering the jobs and investment that it brings, as well as violate free trade agreements. Regulation can, for instance, cause cost inflation or delay the execution of projects. Therefore, for a new and emerging oil and gas economy, Guyana should apply the following five fundamental principles to achieve effective local-content policies:

- **Know where the value is and where the jobs are:** The first imperative is for policy makers to gain detailed knowledge of the resources supply chain so that they understand where total value is in terms of revenue and employment.
- **Understand the competitive edge:** The spending that can be captured locally varies significantly among countries due to a number of factors, including the type of resource, the level of industrialisation, the country's unique aspects such as location and language, and whether other industries have a significant presence.
- **Carefully assess the opportunity cost of regulatory intervention:** When governments impose local-content requirements, they must carefully assess whether regulations are too unwieldy for companies, unnecessarily raising costs, potentially causing significant delays and damaging competitiveness. They should also guard against creating perverse incentives.
- **Don't just regulate, enable:** Most resource-driven countries devote too little attention to creating an environment that supports the achievement of local content targets. Government can assist in a number of areas, from helping to develop skills to providing financing and coordinating local suppliers.
- **Carefully track and enforce progress:** Making procedures simple to administer and track, appointing a credible regulator with enforcement power, and creating a regulatory body that can coordinate efforts are crucial to making progress on local content.

Private companies play an essential role in the development of local content. It is crucial for companies to have a detailed understanding of their future spending profile and the local supplier base; to organise effectively to achieve their local-content goals by rooting them deeply in company processes for procurement and human resources rather than corporate social responsibility; to engage proactively with the Government as they make local-content policy decisions; and to support the development of local supply chains through targeted skill-building, and research and development programmes.

Spending the windfall

There is a broad range of approaches for Guyana to use resource revenues. It can invest the money abroad or use it to repay foreign debt. Guyana can also invest at least a portion of its oil revenue at home in infrastructure and other key areas. A share of revenue can be directed to specific regions for both investment and consumption purposes. The Government can also use resources revenue more generally for domestic needs such as higher wages for public-sector workers, subsidies for energy resources, or other social-welfare programs.

Whilst the best approach may vary somewhat, there are some valuable lessons from international experience to date, that can be broadly apply. Guyana should consider the following if it wants to reap the full benefits of its resource endowments:

- **Set expectations**: In order to counter ill-informed pressure that could lead to wasteful spending, governments need to agree early in the process on the principles for how the resource wealth will be used and manage expectations among their citizens accordingly (Amoako-Tuffour 2011).
- **Ensure spending is transparent and benefits are visible**: Governments need to ensure that institutional mechanisms are put in place for a high level of transparency so that recipients see the benefits of invested resource windfalls.
- **Smooth government expenditure**: Setting a target for the non-commodity government budget balance can insulate public expenditures from volatility. During periods of relatively high commodity prices or output, the overall budget might accumulate a surplus, while during periods of low prices or output it might run a deficit but leave spending intact (International Monetary Fund 2009).
- **Keep government lean**: Resource-driven countries often suffer from bloated government bureaucracies. Such effects reduce not only public-sector productivity but also incentives for working in the private

sector, inhibiting wider economic development. Hence, Guyana should actively seek to keep the public sector in proportion by regularly comparing ratios for each function with those of other countries. It should also consider how it can consistently recognise duplicative structures in the public sector that could be consolidated. One method to keep pay consistent is to benchmark wages to similar jobs in the private sector and to assign public-sector roles a 'clean wage' without hidden perks or privileges (McKinsey Center for Government 2012).

- **Shift from consumption to investment**: Channelling some of the resource wealth into domestic investment and savings is crucial to start transforming natural resource wealth into long-term prosperity. Establishing institutional mechanisms to support this process can be useful, because they can address any bias toward government consumption spending and deficits, enhance fiscal discipline, and raise the quality of debate and scrutiny.
- **Boost domestic capabilities to use funds well**: Resource-driven governments need to ensure the development of strong investment capabilities in the public sector. The International Monetary Fund (IMF) and the World Bank jointly produce an index of public investment efficiency, enabling countries to track progress in this area (Dabla-Norris et al 2010). Some of the key areas to address include project appraisal, selection, implementation and auditing.

Economic development

Very few resource-driven countries have sustained strong Gross Domestic Product (GDP) growth for longer than a decade. Even those that have appeared to put their economics on a healthier longer-term growth trajectory have rarely managed to transform that growth into broader economic prosperity.

However, doing so is not impossible. One major imperative for Guyana is to focus on removing barriers to productivity across five key areas of the economy: the resources sector itself; resource rider sectors such as utilities and construction; manufacturing; local services such as retail trade and financial services; and agriculture.

Local services, which include hospitality, telecommunications, and financial sectors, are often seen as the indirect beneficiaries of the resource booms. These sectors can achieve large productivity improvements, which can often result in significant growth in GDP and employment, but these sectors are often overlooked by policy makers. Removing microeconomic barriers can significantly increase productivity and economic growth for an emerging economy such as Guyana.

References

Amoako-Tuffour, J. (2011), *Public Participation in the Making of Ghana's Petroleum Revenue Management Law* [Homepage of Natural Resource Charter Technical Advisory Group], [Online]. Available: https://resourcegovernance.org/sites/default/files/documents/ghana-public-participation.pdf [Accessed: 24 February 2019].

Chandler, J.A.P. (2018). *Petroleum Resource Management: How Governments Manage Their Offshore Petroleum Resources,* Edward Elgar Publishing, Cheltenham, UK.

Dobbs, R., Oppenheim, J., Kendall, A., Thompson, F., Bratt, M., van der Marel, F. (2013), *Reverse the curse: Maximizing the potential of resource-driven economies* [Homepage of McKinsey Global Institute], [Online]. Available:

https://www.mckinsey.com/industries/metals-and-mining/our-insights/reverse-the-curse-maximizing-the-potential-of-resource-driven-economies [Accessed: 25 February 2018].

Dabla-norris, E., Brumby, J., Kyobe, A., et al (2012). "Investing in public investment: an index of public investment efficiency", *Journal of Economic Growth,* vol. 17, no. 3, pp. 235-266.

Gebre, B., Hallman, P., et al (2012), *Transforming government performance through lean management* [Homepage of McKinsey Centre for Government], [Online]. Available: https://www.mckinsey.com/~/media/mckinsey/dotcom/client_servic e/Public%20Sector/PDFS/MCG_Transforming_through_lean_mana gement.ashx [Accessed: 25 February 2019].

Schaechter, A., Caceres, C., et al (2009), *Fiscal Rules - Anchoring Expectations for Sustainable Public Finances* [Homepage of International Monetary Fund], [Online]. Available: https://www.imf.org/external/np/pp/eng/2009/121609.pdf [Accessed: 25 February 2019].

Schwab, K. (2012), *The Global Competitiveness Report 2012-2013* [Homepage of World Economic Forum], [Online]. Available:

https://www.weforum.org/reports/global-competitiveness-report-2012-2013 [Accessed: 23 February 2019]

About the contributor

Bobby Gossai, Jr. is currently researching a PhD in Economics at the University of Aberdeen focusing on fiscal terms and regulations for an emerging oil-producing country in a volatile price environment. His background is energy and petroleum economics as applied to various models of oil price behaviour and general oil structures. His professional experiences include being the head of the Guyana Oil and Gas Association; the senior policy analyst and advisor at the Ministry of Natural Resources and Environment; senior analyst at the Ministry of Agriculture; economist at the National Competitiveness Strategy Unit; and a national accounts statistician at the Bureau of Statistics.

Chapter 14

From Raleigh to Liza – the quest for riches

There are many challenges ahead, says Frank Anthony, but they can be overcome

Sir Walter Raleigh's 1595 book, *The discoverie of the large, rich and bewtiful empire of Guiana, with a relation of the Great and Golden Citie of Manoa (which the Spaniards call El Dorado)*, created the myth that the fantastical city of Manoa was located in Guiana.

For years explorers combed the interior looking for the mythical city. Several areas were identified, with Pirara, in the Rupununi becoming the focus of attention. In 1842, the British sent soldiers from the West Indian regimen to establish a fort (New Guiana) and protect the area. But, alas the search for the elusive Golden City remained inconclusive.

Not far from Pirara is the Takatu Basin, and in 1910 another search started here, this time for the 'black gold'. By 1916 the first well was sunk, and so began Guyana's quest to find oil. However, this and much of other onshore efforts remained unsuccessful or commercially unviable. Offshore efforts seemed to mirror this lack of success initially, with failings such as the Shell exploration in the Abary 1(1975), Total exploration in the Arapaima #1 (1990) and CGX exploration at Eagle (2000), Horseshoe (2005).

However, offshore explorers' fortune changed, when on 15 May 2015, the ExxonMobil operator found oil at a depth of 18,730 feet (5,700 feet of water), 120 miles off the coast of Guyana. The discovery of oil at Liza 1, was soon followed by others at Liza 2, Liza 3, Liza 4, Liza Deep, Snoek-1, Payara-1, Payara-2, Turbot 1, Ranger, Tilapia 1 and Haimara 1. The current estimated total recoverable gross resources for the blocks is more than five billion barrels of oil equivalent. This projection would change as more analysis is done on the reserves, especially given the last two discoveries which are considered among the four most high impact discoveries of oil and gas globally so far for 2019.

These findings have placed Guyana on a fast track to becoming an oil-rich economy. Considering Liza 1 and 2 wells only, the International Monetary Fund has estimated that the maximum annual revenue at peak production is expected to be $2.5bn (all figures in US dollars) in 2028 with the total government revenue over the lifespan of the field (s) being $26.7bn (Liza 1 and 2). A much more conservative projection by Open Oil put this number at between $7bnn (Liza 1 only) to $18bn (Liza 1 and 2) over the life of the well. It is estimated that between 2025 to 2028 revenues could peak at $800m to $3.9bn per year. This would have the effect of doubling the Guyanese economy.

But are these discoveries a blessing or a curse? The answer to this question is that it could be either; depending on how we manage our resources.

There is much that can be learned from the experience of other countries. We have witnessed the pre-source curse; an affliction wherein the government of a country embarks on overspending and borrowing based on the promise of oil wealth, we have seen volatility which occurs when the economy of a country is held at the whim of oil prices, and we have seen the Dutch Disease, where inflation or exchange rate appreciation makes other exports uncompetitive.

We must remember too, that these oil and gas resources are non-renewable, and the wealth generated now must be used for this and future generations.

If we can avoid these pitfalls, then the funds will surely be a blessing.

For Guyanese to ensure that these resources are utilised wisely, there is an urgent need to develop a vision and a strategy for the oil and gas sector. To produce such a vision would require a multi-stakeholder approach, where everyone with interest can join the discussion to fashion a national position on the oil and gas sector.

To implement this vision, we must create new institutions, develop new laws, policies and regulations, train human resources to work in the industry, and create access to funding and know how to help companies align to produce goods and services for the new sector.

The Government needs to develop new institutions for the oil and gas sector quickly. This includes a Ministry of Oil and Gas, which would drive legislation, policies and regulation in the industry. This Ministry must have the legal, economic, audit, and scientific capacity to provide expert guidance to government decision-making in the industry. There is a need for the establishment of additional institutions, such as contemplated by the new laws, and to monitor activities that are currently ongoing with both explorations, and establishing the prerequisites for first oil.

The country needs to develop a suite of laws and policies for the oil and gas sector. The work required to be done on our legislation varies, in some cases, we may need to simply update existing laws, but in others, the creation of entirely new laws; which detail the specifics of exploration activities, production activities and post-production activities is necessary.

In addition to the laws which will specify the logistics of how oil and gas mining should be done, there is an urgent need to update the laws which are concerned with the safety of human resources and the environment. We need to ensure that there is legislation that protects the unique aquatic environment that Guyana's waters provide, and we need to ensure that flora and fauna of areas in the vicinity of the drilling are protected as well. We also need to upgrade our occupational and safety standards to comply with international standards.

So far very little attention has been given to these types of legislation, policies and regulations.

The Government has spent most of its time up to this point working on Guyana's version of a sovereign wealth fund called the Natural Resource Fund Act.

Important legislation such as this should have bipartisan inputs and should take into consideration the concerns of the private sector, the Opposition, and key stakeholder groups.

While the intent of the legislation is welcome, the devil is in the details such as concerns for the independence of the fund, the membership of the fund, and the fiscal rule that would be used to trigger the fund.

The Government enacted this legislation without the participation of the Opposition, which turns it into a subject of controversy. Since the unilateral enactment of the law, the institutions that are required to be implemented is yet to be established. These issues must be properly sorted out before petroleum funds start flowing to the Natural Resource Fund.

There has been a lack of leadership on local content in the oil and gas industry. This indifference on the part of the Government is hurting local businesses and the country's strategic interests. There is a vacuum where there should be leaders formulating legislation, policies and regulations regarding local content.

Experiences around the world have been varied depending on those countries peculiar context. These experiences must not paralyse us into doing nothing – we need to act to create opportunities for our local businesses. It is critical at this point, to bring together the private sector, the international oil companies, and international consulting experts and government so that we might develop local content for the oil and gas sector.

Through these consultations, a fair balance can be struck where everyone wins. In addition to this facilitation, the Government should support companies to realign themselves to work for the oil and gas industry. This support should include access to know how, to capital, and other support services for them to become contractors or subcontractors to Exxon Mobil and its affiliates.

The Government should also develop short-, medium- and long-term human resource strategies for the oil and gas sector. In the near term, there should be a policy of encouraging skilled Guyanese from around the world to return home and to work in the industry. Additionally, the Government should facilitate the establishment of an oil and gas school which can produce skilled persons who are necessary for working offshore. In the medium, to long term, government and the industry should map the human resource requirements, and offer scholarships to young Guyanese in engineering, accounting, legal, economic modelling, geology etc.

The Government needs to urgently establish a fully functioning and equipped oil and gas research institution that would be capable of monitoring activities within the oil and gas sector and to evaluate the country oil and gas reserves. These institutions will help to ensure better governance and transparency in the industry. It would also allow policymakers to have access to an independent data source to be used when formulating policies and decisions.

Further, the Government must improve on their current contract management capacity. There is a need for timely review to see whether the obligations stipulated under the contract is appropriately met. A critical component of managing recoverable expenditures is to have the auditing capacity to handle and interpret the cost recovery submissions and external auditing information.

In establishing a new sector, there will always be teething problems. But if there is a willingness to learn, and work in the country's interests, these challenges can be overcome.

While there have been expensive missteps and blunders, we need to learn quickly and put the strategies in place so that this and the future generation of Guyanese will benefit from the blessings of black gold.

As Raleigh had suspected all these years, Guyana has lots of riches, but in the end, you have to know where to look and how to manage it. Liza much like gold shines with the promise of hope to our people. However, it is still anybody's guess whether the black gold will be managed well enough to propel Guyana's prosperity through the 21st century.

About the contributor

Dr Frank C. S. Anthony is the former Minister of Culture Youth and Sports. He is a graduate from the Russian Friendship University in Medicine and has a Master's Degree in Public Health from the Hebrew University in Israel. He also lectures at the University of Guyana in Epidemiology. He is a Member of Parliament and an Executive and Central Committee Member of the People's Progressive Party. He was recently appointed the Pan-Caribbean Partnership against HIV and Aids (PANCAP) Champion of Change.

Chapter 15

The whole picture – oil and gas exploration in the Caribbean

A prosperous roadmap can be put in place for the whole region, says Anthony T. Bryan, but very careful management is the key

There is a mad rush for the 'frontier provinces' of oil and gas in the Caribbean. Encouraged by the massive discoveries in Guyana since 2015 a number of international oil companies (IOCs) and state companies (NOCs) are rushing to tie up acreage in bid rounds in the expectation that their investments will eventually pay off.

Countries in the Circum-Caribbean region have opened their territorial waters to deepwter exploration for oil and gas. Is the Caribbean poised to become a new, and not mythical El Dorado for oil and gas? It's early 2019 and time for a reality check!

French Guiana is the country that inspired the Caribbean momentum in deepwater exploration. It began following the discovery of the Zaedyus well by UK exploration company Tullow Energy in late 2011. The Zaedyus well substantiated the theory of Tullow geologists that the geological features offshore Ghana (where the huge Jubilee field had been discovered in 2007) are replicated on the opposite side of the Atlantic, in the now named Guyana-Suriname Basin (GSB). In 2011 French Guiana was actually the hottest of the deepwater 'frontier provinces' – the P10 (10 per cent probability) reserve estimate of the Zaedyus is 840m barrels of oil equivalent (boe).

In 2013 I reported on the dash for deepwater oil and gas in the countries of the wider Caribbean. (Bryan, 2013). But with the exception of Trinidad and Tobago, which is a mature oil province with 105 years of production and where 39 deepwater blocs (12,000 feet to 19,000 feet) were marked at that time for exploration and oil plays, there was not much optimism about a deepwater oil and gas future for the Caribbean region. The plunge in oil prices starting in 2014 hurt the finances of oil-producing countries such as Trinidad, but it did not dampen the enthusiasm for regional oil exploration since most IOCs are in the business for the long run.

Why is there this renewed interest in Caribbean oil and gas?

The development of technology to facilitate the exploration and developing of hydrocarbon resources in deep water has resulted in the interest shown in the countries of the Caribbean region. The recent geological surveys demonstrate that the region consists of a series of structural elements, the most prominent being the Venezuelan and Colombian deep sea sub-oceanic depressions, the Nicaraguan Rise, and the Greater and Lesser Antilles bordering the Caribbean Sea in the North and East.

In a 2012 report, the US Geological Survey of 31 priority geological provinces in South America and the Caribbean assessed the undiscovered conventional hydrocarbon potential at 126bn barrels of crude oil and 679trn cubic feet (tcf) of natural gas. In the Guyana-Suriname Basin the crude oil potential was assessed at 13.6bn barrels and natural gas at 21tcf. (USGS, 2012)

Guyana

The impressive hydrocarbon discoveries in Guyana's deep water since 2015 have validated the findings of the US Geological Survey. The IOCs Exxon and Hess announced more than two billion barrels in new discoveries offshore of Guyana at the end of 2018 increasing their overall recoverable resources in the region to about five billion barrels of oil equivalent. Guyana's oil production is expected to begin in 2020 at a rate of 120,000 barrels per day (bpd). There are still 17 more prospects to drill, so Guyana's crude production could reach a potential 750,000 bpd by 2025. It will easily surpass Trinidad's oil production and could move ahead of Venezuela and Mexico if they do not address their current production declines.

But it's not a smooth path. Guyana faces some practical challenges. The country is new to hydrocarbon resource development and has to continue to develop strategic plans that may include establishing a state energy company with associated legislation, as well as laws for hydrocarbon extraction, fiscal regimes, state participation, operating agreements such as PSAs, and environmental protection statutes among other measures. Available expertise from Trinidad and Tobago, Mexico, Canada, other producer nations, and a number of international agencies are contributing to this transition.

There are other hurdles to overcome. These are mostly above ground issues including: unresolved border and territorial disputes (with Venezuela and Suriname), and management of the potential windfall (mainly the absorptive capacity of a small population faced with potential wealth).

Guyana's relative period of political stability over the past two decades was jeopardized in December 2018 by the defection of a member of the one vote majority of the APNU-AFC coalition in the National Assembly that resulted in the fall of the current government and a call for new elections.

The above ground risks will require studied responses, and in some cases diplomatic resolution. The major threat is the maritime border claim by Venezuela of sovereignty over Guyana's EEZ. Guyana is pursuing a judicial settlement to the matter at the level of the International Court of Justice. In 2019 the longer-term risk is that political implosion in Venezuela could provoke increased military pressure on Guyana's border from a desperate political regime.

French Guiana

In French Guiana expectations of a boom have given away to disappointment. After the Zaedyus find in 2011 four other appraisal wells were unsuccessful. A partnership of Shell, Tullow, Northpet and Wessek Exploration has so far failed to discover commercial hydrocarbons in French Guiana's exploration acreage. It is difficult to predict the results of future activities.

Suriname

While there is abundant oil in Guyana's offshore fields in the GSB, nothing of significance has been found as yet in offshore Suriname. Kosmos Energy has hit two dry holes in a row. Experts say that analyses of prospects offshore Suriname still look favourable. Exploration continues apace with joint venture partners that are looking at prospects in Block 42 that will be tested in 2020. (OilNow, October 2018)

Suriname's expected windfall may simply be a matter of time and more investment. Over the past 35 years, the country has produced oil from a small number of onshore wells, and in the event of successful offshore oil plays, in its deepwater province of 150,000 square km, it is well prepared.

The regulatory system for oil and gas has been in place for many years, and unlike Guyana, the country has most of the resident skills, and the local negotiating capacity to deal with the IOCs. The state oil company Staatsolie has been in the business of attracting exploration and production (E&P) contracts, offering bids, and negotiating production sharing contracts (PSCs) since 2004. The company is both the regulator and market participant.

Trinidad and Tobago

Trinidad and Tobago (T&T) the Caribbean's major oil, natural gas, and LNG producer had to face the full brunt of the global fall in oil and natural gas prices that began in 2014. Despite the volatility of energy prices, increased costs, and tighter environmental standards, the major oil and gas companies in T&T have adopted new technologies for land and offshore exploration, as well as additional investments to keep the industry resilient.

Trinidad is a natural gas economy that services large multiple locally-based world class competitive industries including methanol, ethanol, aluminium, and ammonium sulphate. Gas production is on the rise and expectations are that gas production will stabilise over the period 2020 to 2023 at approximately four billion cubic feet per day based on the level of investment to be undertaken by upstream companies and cross border sharing agreements with Venezuela for the 14 trillion cubic feet of natural gas available to both countries.

But the situation is tenuous. If the Maduro Government in Venezuela does not survive the current political impasse, the planned cross-border investments and energy sharing agreements with T&T may be in doubt.

Other Caribbean countries

As a consequence of Guyana's fortunes, major upstream companies are exploring for hydrocarbons in the territorial waters of Barbados, Grenada, Jamaica, The Bahamas and Haiti. Other than Guyana and Barbados, the prospects are mixed or uncertain. But T&T with its experience, technical expertise, capacity and multiple service companies has signed MOUs with the Governments of Guyana and Grenada and is negotiating a similar agreement with Barbados.

The Caribbean's future

At present, the deep-water exploration in the Southern Caribbean and the 'Three Guianas' (Guyana French Guiana and Suriname) is not a recipe for hyperbole. Rather it is an opportunity for us to design the roadmaps for regional prosperity.

First, the potential for unequal distribution of revenue from energy rents is great, and movement toward the 'resource curse' is almost certain, unless watchdogs such as the Extractive Industries Transparency Initiative (EITI) are entrenched from the beginning, and proper sovereign wealth (heritage and stabilisation) funds are established promptly.

Second, this is an opportunity to fund rapid diversification into renewable energy (RE) even though fossil fuels will be present for the foreseeable future.

Third, Trinidad and Tobago and Guyana should take a leadership role in advancing a regional sustainable energy future that requires a holistic vision of regional energy cooperation. It would integrate our regional energy policy with trade, economics, environment, security, foreign relations and geopolitical considerations, while extending the dialogue with producing and consuming countries alike.

Finally, leaders and the public should be made aware that energy revenue earned must transcend political cycles and generations. Abundant natural resources will do little to promote economic development without sound economic management, and a willingness to address the political factors that may conflict with sound policy choices.

References

Bryan, Anthony T. (April 11, 2013). The Dash for Deepwater Oil and Gas in the Caribbean: What's at the Finish Line?
http://www.petroleumworld.com/lagniappe13041101.htm

OilNow, October 13, 2018. https://oilnow.gy/featured/oil-galore-in-guyana-but-not-a-drop-found-yet-offshore-suriname/

U.S. Geological Survey (USGS 2012). Assessment of Undiscovered Conventional Oil and Gas Resources of South America and the Caribbean, 2012. https://pubs.usgs.gov/fs/2012/3046/fs2012-3046.pdf

About the contributor

Professor Anthony T. Bryan, Ph.D. is an honorary senior fellow with the Institute of International Relations at the University of the West Indies, St. Augustine, Trinidad and Tobago, where he was the professor/director for a decade, and a senior associate of the Center for Strategic and International Studies (CSIS) in Washington DC. He has been a consultant on Caribbean energy for a dozen years.

Poem: Rainforest Interlude

Grace Nichols

Nothing then, put to seek refuge
from the chaos of Stabroek Market Square
and the melting gold of the El Dorado-sun
and dive into the cool ambiance
of the Georgetown Museum – surfacing
among the glass cabinets of its stilled creation
drawn from the artistry of forest trees and rivers.
Like walking swimmers, we reacquaint with;
Aripiama world's biggest fresh water fish,
Great Harpy-eagle, the startling, Hoatzin bird
and standing where my childhood left him,
old gold-seeking, gold-toothed, Pork-knocker,
saucepan and cutlass still hanging from his waist
still ready to cut his way through rainforest.

About the contributor

Grace Nichols was born and educated in Guyana and has written widely for both adults and children. Among her awards, are The Commonwealth Poetry Prize for her first collection, *I is a long-memoried Woman* and The Guyana Poetry Prize for *Sunris*. She was poet-in-residence at the Tate Gallery in London and is one of the poets on the current GCSE English syllabus in Britain.

Bite-Sized Public Affairs Books are designed to provide insights and stimulating ideas that affect us all in, for example, journalism, social policy, education, government and politics.

They are deliberately short, easy to read, and authoritative books written by people who are either on the front line or who are informed observers. They are designed to stimulate discussion, thought and innovation in all areas of public affairs. They are all firmly based on personal experience and direct involvement and engagement.

The most successful people all share an ability to focus on what really matters, keeping things simple and understandable. When we are faced with a new challenge most of us need quick guidance on what matters most, from people who have been there before and who can show us where to start. As Stephen Covey famously said, "The main thing is to keep the main thing, the main thing."

But what exactly is the main thing?

Bite-Sized books were conceived to help answer precisely that question crisply and quickly and, of course, be engaging to read, written by people who are experienced and successful in their field.

The brief? Distil the 'main things' into a book that can be read by an intelligent non-expert comfortably in around 60 minutes. Make sure the book enables the reader with specific tools, ideas and plenty of examples drawn from real life. Be a virtual mentor.

We have avoided jargon – or explained it where we have used it as a shorthand – and made few assumptions about the reader, except that they are literate and numerate, involved in understanding social policy, and that they can adapt and use what we suggest to suit their own, individual purposes. Most of all the books are focused on understanding and exploiting the changes that we witness every day but which come at us in what seems an incoherent stream.

They can be read straight through at one easy sitting and then referred to as necessary – a trusted repository of hard-won experience.

Bite-Sized Books Catalogue

Business Books

Ian Benn
Write to Win
How to Produce Winning Proposals and RFP Responses
Matthew T Brown
Understand Your Organisation
An Introduction to Enterprise Architecture Modelling
David Cotton
Rethinking Leadership
Collaborative Leadership for Millennials and Beyond
Richard Cribb
IT Outsourcing: 11 Short Steps to Success
An Insider's View
Phil Davies
How to Survive and Thrive as a Project Manager
The Guide for Successful Project Managers
Paul Davies
Developing a Business Case
Making a Persuasive Argument out of Your Numbers
Paul Davies
Developing a Business Plan
Making a Persuasive Plan for Your Business
Paul Davies
Contract Management for Non-Specialists
Paul Davies
Developing Personal Effectiveness in Business
Paul Davies
A More Effective Sales Team
Sales Management Focused on Sales People

Maiqi Ma
> Win with China
>> Acclimatisation for Mutual Success Doing Business with China

Elena Mihajloska
> Bridging the Virtual Gap
>> Building Unity and Trust in Remote Teams

Rob Morley
> Agile in Business
>> A Guide for Company Leadership

Gillian Perry
> Managing the People Side of Change
>> Ten Short Steps to Success in IT Outsourcing

Saibal Sen
> Next Generation Service Management
>> An Analytics Driven Approach

Don Sharp
> Nothing Happens Until You Sell Something
>> A Personal View of Selling Techniques

Christopher Hosford
> Great Business Meetings! Greater Business Results
>> Transforming Boring Time-Wasters into Dynamic Productivity Engines

Lifestyle Books

Anna Corthout
> Alive Again
>> My Journey to Recovery

Phil Davies
> Don't Worry Be Happy
>> A Personal Journey

Phil Davies
> Feel the Fear and Pack Anyway
>> Around the World in 284 Days

Stuart Haining
> My Other Car is an Aston
>> A Practical Guide to Ownership and Other Excuses to Quit Work and Start a Business

Bill Heine
Cancer – Living Behind Enemy Lines Without a Map
Regina Kerschbaumer
Yoga Coffee and a Glass of Wine
A Yoga Journey
Gillian Perry
Capturing the Celestial Lights
A Practical Guide to Imagining the Northern Lights
Arthur Worrell
A Grandfather's Story
Arthur Worrell's War

Public Affairs Books

Eben Black
Lies Lunch and Lobbying
PR, Public Affairs and Political Engagement – A Guide
John Mair and Richard Keeble (Editors)
Investigative Journalism Today:
Speaking Truth to Power
John Mair, Richard Keeble and Farrukh Dhondy (Editors)
V.S Naipaul:
The legacy
Christian Wolmar
Wolmar for London
Creating a Grassroots Campaign in a Digital Age
John Mair and Neil Fowler (Editors)
Do They Mean Us – Brexit Book 1
The Foreign Correspondents' View of the British Brexit

Fiction

Paul Davies
The Ways We Live Now
Civil Service Corruption, Wilful Blindness, Commercial
Fraud, and Personal Greed – a Novel of Our Times
Paul Davies
Coming To
A Novel of Self-Realisation

Children's Books

Chris Reeve – illustrations by Mike Tingle
>The Dictionary Boy
>>A Salutary Tale

Fredrik Payedar
>The Spirit of Chaos
>>It Begins

Made in the USA
Columbia, SC
13 September 2019